The Totaled Woman

The Totaled Woman

True Slices of Life
from a Mother of Five

By Marcia Veldhuis

VMI Publishers
Sisters, Oregon

The Totaled Woman:
True Slices of Life from a Mother of Five
© 2009 by Marcia Veldhuis
All rights reserved. Published 2009.

Published by
VMI Publishers
Sisters, Oregon
www.vmipublishers.com

ISBN: 1-935265-17-2
ISBN 13: 978-1-035265-17-7
Library of Congress Control Number: 2009939368

Printed in the USA.

Illustrations by the author

Cover and interior design by Juanita Dix

Table of Contents

Preface

These stories are true, totally true. There are perhaps some writers who would feel the need to pad truth with fiction, or put several stories together as one to make that one seem more fantastical. This has never been needed in our home! Day-to-day living has always been stranger than fiction!

Dedication

I dedicate this book

to Johannes

and to Nathan, Ingrid, Olivia, Stefan and Alisson

And

to Dr. James Dobson

whose wisdom and advice

has kept me sane and on the right track.

—— Best of All Creation ——

The gentle stream meandered like a lazy snake –
A sparkling gurgling ribbon flowing brownish-blue.
It slithers on amongst the daisies as they wake,
With fragile fingers circling golden orbs in dew;
Their little faces puckered, spreading smiles heavenward.

The craggy cliffs plunge downward to the ocean swells
With just a Word behemoth freely roams the land.
The rising brilliance of day's ruler morning tells;
Yes, sun and moon and stars shine forth at His command.
Created grandeur shouts in praises heavenward.

Sweet little toes now wriggle in the gentle stream
That slithers through the smiling daisies on its way.
The child's eyes the mighty mountain peaks esteem.
Her mother sees the little girl, her child at play:
The best of all creation. Thanks waft heavenward.

—— No Rest in Heaven ——

"Naptime!" The younger children were finally asleep, and our four-year-old was resisting the rest time that his mother desperately needed him to have.

His big brown eyes were thinking deep thoughts. "Mommy, when I go to Heaven, do I have to stay there forever?"

Oh, I knew what the correct answer should be: *When you get to Heaven, you will want to stay forever.* But that is not a four-year-old answer. I don't really comprehend that answer myself, so how would my little boy?

"Nathan, you don't **have** to stay there forever if it would make you sad, because there is only joy in Heaven! We are never even tired, or need to rest there."

"Well, Mom," he continued earnestly as I tucked him into bed, "I might want to stay; so…there are no beds in Heaven?"

That's it – no need for naps in Heaven…and no tired mothers either.

—— A Feathery Kibble ——

So, shall I regale you with my morning so far? I awoke to twittering birds about 6:00, and decided to just snooze a bit, since Johannes is out of town. About 6:45, I heard a cat-sized "THUMP" on the back porch. Assuming Saddam was on the loose, with the extra time on his paws this morning, I reluctantly arose to feed the beasts.

As I approached the door from the laundry room into the garage, I heard Bilbo (alias Saddam) jump through the dog door. He and a frantic bird greeted Bandit and me as I opened the door. The bird was screeching, and tried to come into the house. Fortunately, I was standing there and it flew into the garage - with Bandit in hot pursuit - woofing and bounding about in a most non-catching manner.

Bilbo just sauntered into the house whining for his kibbled. Oh, one other thing...the headlights were on in my car...and my seat is filled with cat hair. I'm still trying to figure out how Bilbo managed to turn the light switch.

Ah yes, another day in the life of Marcia...and all that before 7 a.m.

—— Total Body Immersion ——

I sent Nathan downstairs with two plastic gallons of milk, which needed to go in the downstairs refrigerator. We have two refrigerators because we have five children, and five gallons will just not fit in one! Being almost 12, and on the verge of testosterone surge, Nathan headed for the stairs balancing one gallon on each palm, holding them up at head level as if he were a waiter in a fancy restaurant. Unfortunately, his balance went awry as did the two gallons of milk. Fortunately, the stairs were not carpeted; although from Nathan's point of view, I suppose that was unfortunate, since the stairs — once wet — were slippery. Clean-up was definitely easier without carpet.

Nathan descended at a precipitous rate in a cascade of white foamy liquid. Thankfully, there were only six steps to the slate floor of the foyer. It may have been a hard trip down, but it wasn't fatal. He survived with surprisingly little personal damage, but the cleanup was an awesome task. Milk had splashed all over the foyer, even up to the ceiling. Perceptions change as we get older, and Stefan (age four) was thrilled with the clean-up detail. Nathan was a good sport, and worked diligently to mop up the mess, with Stefan's enthusiastic — if ineffective — assistance.

Of course, by the end, both boys were covered in milk and water, and needed a shower. Now, they had never showered together before, but this seemed like a good time to try it…wrong…

The girls and I were finishing up the cleaning of the stairs and foyer when I could no longer ignore the wild screaming and laughing coming from the

4   The Totaled Woman

downstairs bathroom. Now, entering the bathroom of a near-teen is risky, but my motherly instinct told me this was one of those acceptable times. As I opened the door, bubbles gushed everywhere. Behind the shower curtain were the perpetrators of the biggest shampoo fight I have ever witnessed. Each boy had a squeeze-bottle of shampoo, and was squirting it at the other as if it were ketchup!

Believe me, ketchup would have been preferable. Those two boys were so slippery, it was almost impossible to grab hold of them. Never doubt the abilities of a desperate mother; I managed to get them out of the shower, turn off the water, and dry them off. Of course, both boys were still coated in a layer of slippery shampoo, but at that point, I didn't care. A little lingering soap never hurt anyone. As the two naked boys attempted to escape the scene of the crime, I managed to give each a smart smack on the unprotected backside. I started upstairs with naked little Stefan wrapped in a towel, sobbing pathetically, leaving Nathan downstairs to find his own clothes, and restore his dignity.

As I reached the foyer, which was still wet from our milk escapade, I found Ingrid and Olivia chatting with a perfect stranger! As I look back on it, I suppose the man figured he had stumbled on the house of some insane mother torturing her children – the screaming had been prodigious, and I had no idea how long he'd been in the house. Not only was I soaking wet from retrieving the boys, but I was covered in bubbles from head to foot. Little Stefan sized up this new situation, and with wisdom beyond his years, scampered off to his room, where he dressed himself and remained playing quietly until the latest crisis had passed.

I took one look at this strange man, put my outstretched hand on his chest, and pushed him gently toward the door. "Excuse me for a moment, please." I said as calmly as I could manage. He backed out the door, which I shut in his face. I can't imagine what went through his mind as he watched through the window in the door as I bawled out the girls for opening the door to a perfect stranger. As the girls ran crying to their rooms, I opened the door again, still having no idea who this person was, and asked him what I could do for him.

He was a post-doctoral candidate, coming to interview for a position in Dr. Veldhuis' lab. A month or so before, Johannes had mentioned his coming, but we never discussed it again, and I had totally forgotten about it. Somewhere in my muddled memory (a condition exacerbated by total-body-immersion in shampoo), I remembered that this person was having dinner with us and spending the night. The memory of the rest of the evening has vanished. Needless to say, the gentleman did not take the position.

—— Long-Distance Coordinator ——

The phone rang. "Hey, Mom, we can't find Dad. Do you know where he is?" That might be a normal question for our kids to ask; after all, perhaps their father had to run an errand, or had gone for a walk...

In this case, the children ranged in age from 17 to 25. They were with their dad in Virginia at Christopher Newport University to watch Stefan's soccer game. I was home in Rochester, Minnesota.

"I assume he is with you at the hotel," I responded.

"Well, he is, but we're supposed to meet him in the parking lot to go to the game. He doesn't answer his cell phone, and he isn't here, and the game starts in an hour!"

"Okay, stay where you are; I'll find him. He'll be right there."

So, I called the hotel (long-distance, of course) and asked the front desk to search their lobby for a freckled fellow with glasses, reams of medical papers and a glass of bubbly water. "Yes, we see him," the hotel clerk replied.

"Would you please tell him that his kids are waiting for him in the parking lot?" I know their father well.

—— A Hard Beginning ——

This morning I got up at the usual time, fed the dogs and cat, took the puppy outside, started the coffee…the most important ingredient in the morning's ritual…

Since I always get it ready the night before, all I needed to do was pour the water into the coffee maker. That would have been fine, except one of the kids called as I was grinding the beans last night, and I never actually put the ground coffee in the filter or placed the filter it in its place in the coffee maker. So, the first pot of coffee was merely hot water.

I started over: drew another carafe of water, and poured it into the coffee maker…One sip was enough to alert me to a new problem. It now looked like coffee at least, but it tasted like water. What could I have done? I ground the coffee last night, as I always do…perhaps I ground only half the needed coffee beans; I mean, I was distracted by a phone call. I repeated the procedure from the beginning. This time, I knew I'd ground the right amount of coffee and put in the appropriate amount of water – I was set. Nope, colored water again. It was then that I realized the water was flowing through awfully quickly. The little doojiggy through which the water is supposed to be directed slowly into the filter was gone! Oh no! This is garbage day! The doojiggy is in the trash out on the street, stuck in one of the many coffee filters I'd used this morning! I raced out to the trash bin and retrieved the most recent bag of kitchen garbage, sifting through it carefully…ew. After several minutes of pawing through last night's discarded bones, salad and vegetables, as well as several wet, used coffee filters, I happened to glance into the sink, where lay the doojiggy…

While the coffee brewed (doojiggy in place, of course), I attempted to refill the filtered-water container, which was just about empty after the coffee fiasco. I turned on the water at the kitchen sink, and it shot up like a geyser – reaching all the way to one of the chairs in the living room. The metal hose that should be attached to the nozzle had become detached. Fortunately, I had not yet folded the towels in the laundry room, so I just spread them over the lake under the sink and on the significant splashes all around the kitchen and living room.

Perhaps I'll skip the gym this morning. I'm still waiting for a decent cup of coffee.

—— Cleanliness and Godliness ——

I have always prided myself for being an organized person. One day last week I really outdid myself:

1. I checked to make sure Nathan's basketball uniform was clean for that night's game...wrong night.

2. I washed the socks Olivia borrowed from a school chum for PE... Ingrid found them and wore them to school.

3. I wrestled a gigantic ink stain in Johannes' best washable trousers – got it all out...to realize that he had leaned against some acid at work, and taken all color out of the seat of them.

Now, what is it the Bible says about pride?

—— The Eyes Have It ——

I was ready to swim my laps at the pool, but where in the world were my goggles? I emptied the swim bag, but no goggles. "Olivia, have you seen my swim goggles, I thought I left them in my bag, but they aren't here."

"Oh sure, Mom! They are at home in the kitchen. I was peeling the onions for dinner last night and they made my eyes water, so I wore your goggles."

Our gorgeous 5'9' blonde daughter with orange pool goggles, setting out to conquer the onions!

—— All in the Mind ——

I went to church Wednesday night. After all, Johannes was home; everybody was fed, bathed, clothed and in his right mind. So off I went, returning about 8:45. Alisson's pitiful voice whined to me as I walked through the door. As I peeked into her room to say "good night," I noticed that she had a towel spread over her pillow (this is what we do when someone has a queasy tummy, so she won't erp on the pillow.) "Mommy will be right back!" I called, and went to inquire of her father.

Apparently, the Bible story for the evening was some obscure passage from Proverbs, about dragons who vomit and then eat it...delightful. Alisson was sure that she would be sick any minute. It took me almost an hour to calm her childish fears. So much for going to church on Wednesday evenings.

Alisson was so silly to worry about dragons with tummy aches! After all, we more mature types never worry about such silly things...

What is that you are saying, Lord? My worries? But Lord, you don't understand! Those things are worth worrying about...aren't they?

— The Cat Trail —

One fine morning on the day before the church folks joined us at our home for dinner, Ingrid arose early and began her morning's activities. Unbeknownst to her (alas), her shoe (attached to her foot, alas) met with a large amount of evidence of a reprobate feline (in the dining room, alas). Ingrid continued on her rounds: into the kitchen, living room, down the hall and back. She again went into the dining room to collect some more evidence, and actually slid in it; falling down to gather a bit on her pants. Still somehow unaware of her pedal predicament, she headed through the living room, down two sets of stairs, through the downstairs living room and into her own room (we have lovely new beige carpeting…alas).

Only at this point did Ingrid rise to consciousness. With her shoe still on, she walked back upstairs into the foyer and finally took it and her soiled slacks off; leaving them on the carpeted floor.

Always looking for the bright side of a situation, I was at least thankful that the upstairs carpet is cat-poop color. Needless to say, number one daughter was busy for several hours with buckets, brushes, indoor-outdoor vacuum, rags…

How in the world could a person not know she was walking in and spreading cat poop! I mean, wouldn't you think the stench would give you a hint? Maybe it is a good example of walking around in sin…oh nothing really awful, like murder…just little stinky sins like envy, gossip, complaining. After awhile we don't even notice it's there, but we spread it wherever we go.

—— A Murine Morsel ——

Our attack cat brought home another rodent today...either an obese mouse or a mole. Frankly, I didn't inspect it closely. I started into the garage to get a flank steak out of the freezer, when I met Bilbo and his "friend." They were doing a wild fandango on the step. The mouse was lying on its back flailing its legs, and Bilbo was batting it around wildly. I shut the door. After about an hour, the thing disappeared — not under its own power, I'll wager! I thought we were going to have to go out for dinner.

Some people don't do windows, some don't do floors...I don't do mice.

—— Little Painters ——

Today we were painting the fence. It was a fine summer's day in Virginia, with temperatures and humidity both in the 90's. Painting a fence is long, tedious work – especially a white picket fence like ours. This type must be kept up, and painted every couple of years. Why, you ask, did we have such a fence? Ah, therein lies the story.

To explain the fence, I must describe our neighbors, the Krebs. Before we put up the fence, Roy Krebs would stand on the edge of his property facing our yard, while our five kids played soccer, and growl under his breath, "Don't you get that ball in my yard!" The children lost several balls, because once they went in his yard, they were gone forever. So, to save my sanity as well as our balls, we put up the fence. Believe it or not, as Johannes was pounding in the supporting metal stakes necessary to erect the fence, Roy skulked into our yard and tried to pull the first stake out! He said he didn't like the looks of it.

So, today we were going to paint the Krebs' side of the fence. It was a family event, with all seven of us participating. Nathan was not the least bit worried about going into the neighbors' yard, he assured us that he would just tell Mr. Krebs off if he had any complaints!

Ingrid, on the other hand, was consumed with fear. She clutched her paintbrush apprehensively, dabbing it ineffectually first at the paint can, then at the unpainted pickets; all the while glancing furtively toward their house, certain he was coming to get her.

Olivia was very practical in her approach to the project. Actually, she did not appear at the fence for quite awhile, but when she did, she was a sight to behold! She was wearing a long-sleeved hooded sweatshirt, jogging pants, an orange winter stocking cap with "The Gellert Company" emblazoned on the front of it, winter boots and swimming goggles! She was prepared for anything (except perhaps 90-degree heat). To our questions, she replied that she was worried that she might get paint on herself or in her hair. She was a great help, despite her gasping and muttering about the heat.

Stefan didn't want to paint the dumb fence. Mr. Krebs deserved to have his side of the fence just be ugly. He grabbed his paintbrush, plunged it into the white paint, and hurled it across the neighbor's lawn, decorating each blade of grass with bright white.

Alisson was but a toddler, and was just happy to be included in the family project. She began her task by grabbing the only already-freshly-painted picket with her hand, then wiping it (her hand that is) on her shirt, and scratching an itch on her head (all with the paint-hand, of course). She then grabbed the wrong end of the paintbrush lying on top of the paint can. Actually, I believe more paint went on her than she ever applied to the fence.

We were so prepared that day. One was filled with confidence, one crippled by fear, one was angry, one was ignorant; but my favorite was Olivia, who was prepared for anything that came her way. In her own young wisdom, she thought she had it all figured out.

Johannes had attempted to explain what we were going to do and how we were going to accomplish it, but the kids had their own ideas. Of course, if the children had just listened to the wisdom of their father, they would have been better helpers.

Ah, there it is…if we would just listen to the Father…

—— Survival of the Fittest ——

It is always so interesting when Johannes is on a trip. In the two days he's been gone, the shed door blew off (actually it was a bit like Dorothy's house in *The Wizard of Oz* – it sailed into the back yard!); Ingrid wants to know why, at age 14, she may not climb a mountain alone with her boyfriend; the tax assessment on the house arrived – it has increased $34,000 in one year(!); and four-year-old precocious Alisson looked at a corpulent swarthy gentleman at the donut shop and announced - with good volume and excellent pronunciation – "That man looks like a gorilla, Mommy!" Ah the joys of motherhood…

Well, I've re-attached the shed door (I'm pretty handy!); told Ingrid that until she gains some understanding of such things, she can just read my lips… "NO!!" There is absolutely nothing I can do about the taxes; and I *quietly* assured Alisson that the man was probably embarrassed that he looked like a gorilla, and maybe we shouldn't say anything more to make him feel badly.

Sometimes a sense of humor is essential to surviving the day. Imagine what sense of humor the Lord must have to put up with us on a daily basis.

—— A Proverbial Proverb ——

When we were in college, Johannes' roommate, Dave, was a fine Christian fellow who was majoring in math. They are friends to this day.

These two would get into deep conversations, which often excluded those around them. They didn't mean to exclude anyone – they just were unaware – so intellectually demanding were their discussions. One day, the three of us were walking to the college library. The fellows were deep in conversation about what each would say in his valedictory address to the graduating class; I was dutifully walking about 10 paces behind as they strode with gusto toward the double doors of the library. Johannes reached his concluding remarks as they reached the doors. Dave took one door, Johannes the other…they flung them open for me to enter just as Johannes ended his "speech" with, "Many an ass has passed through the gates of Jerusalem!"

Apparently, not all who pass through the halls of learning are worthy of their degrees.

——The Mind Falters——

Tuesday found Nathan ready for his 3:30 soccer game – leaving straight from school for the field – minus one soccer sock. He reminded me a bit of "Diddle Diddle Dumpling My Son John..." as he charged up and down the field with one blue and white sock, and one orange.

Wednesday, Nathan borrowed my sweatshirt because he's lost all of his, and it's cold in the morning leaving for school!

Today is Thursday. Today, Ingrid borrowed my sweatshirt because she got to it before Nathan did, and because it was too far to run downstairs for her coat (which is supposed to hang in the foyer by the door). Today Nathan found his missing soccer sock in the gym during Ingrid's eighth-grade PE class. He discovered my sweatshirt on the floor near the locker room where she'd thrown it, and stuffed the sock in the pocket for safe keeping, planning to retrieve it when Ingrid brought the sweatshirt home after school.

Thursday is a busy day - Nathan's soccer, Stefan's soccer and Ingrid's gymnastics. It is for that reason I require Nathan to deposit his books in the car before leaving for the soccer field, that way we do not forget them.

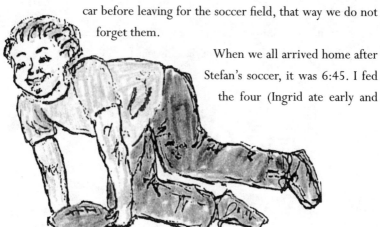

When we all arrived home after Stefan's soccer, it was 6:45. I fed the four (Ingrid ate early and had left for gymnastics with the car pool at 6:00), put Alisson to bed, and left Nathan home to babysit while I ran the car pool home from gymnastics. Johannes was out of town, so this was a one-woman show.

On the way home, Ingrid said, "Oh, I forgot! I have to write an essay on *The Last of the Mohicans!*" It seemed a bit much for a teacher to assign a paper the day before it's due, I observed. To which she responded, "Oh no, Mom, she assigned it last week; I just forgot." Upon arriving home at 8:30, I found Nathan lounging on the couch...no homework done...he had left his book bag in the car.

It is now 10:00 p.m. All are in bed. At 9:30, Nathan called sleepily from under his covers, "Mom, I need my soccer uniform washed by tomorrow morning for our game." As I brought in the clean uniform, I reminded him that there still was only one sock (At this point, I learned about the sock-in-the-pocket trick.). He replied, "Ask Ingrid where she put your sweatshirt." Ingrid grumbled as she left her bed to retrieve the sweatshirt she thought was in the car. She was afraid to go outside alone, thus, Nathan was summoned from beneath the covers, and the two of them went forth.

It was not in the car, and Ingrid confessed that she must have left it "at school somewhere." Nathan flopped back into bed telling his sister how stupid she was to leave her stuff lying all around.

Nathan left his lunchbox at school again today. That dumb Ingrid! How could she be so careless and forget the sweatshirt!

—— Life on a Daily Basis ——

This is one of those days that no one will believe…

Johannes was at a medical meeting in Texas; I was visiting my parents in Idaho; Olivia and Alisson were flying to Arizona the next day to work with their missionary aunt and uncle for two weeks; Stefan was planning an early-morning drive in his father's car to Dulles airport, catching a flight to Oklahoma to visit his girlfriend. Since Nathan and Ingrid no longer were at home, this left the house empty until someone returned.

If we weren't home, you might ask, how do I know what happened. Between the telephone and the fax machine, I had no hope of being spared even one detail.

Stefan's flight was an early one, and it is a one-and-a-half-hour drive from Charlottesville to Dulles, so he was backing out of the driveway by 5 a.m. Now, Stefan is not a morning person, so his friend LJ spent the night at the house to help get him up on time (sisters refused to be involved!). Stefan was up and dressed and in the car on time, but as I mentioned, he is really not much of a morning person, and as he backed out of the garage, he forgot that LJ's car was parked in the driveway…

The impact was sufficient to dislodge our bumper altogether, and do substantial damage to LJ's car. But Stefan had a plane to catch, so he tied the bumper to the car with a couple of leather boot laces, left LJ and the girls asleep, and quietly departed for the airport. The plan was for him to leave the car in a designated area for Johannes to drive home when he returned from his Texas trip.

The first I knew of this debacle was when Olivia called while my parents and I were eating a leisurely breakfast. Stefan had called the house and explained the situation to Olivia, "I'm just now getting on the plane, would you call Dad and tell him not to worry, I've tied the bumper on, and it works fine!" Of course, no one wanted to call Dad at the medical conference and tell him, so they called me…

Olivia was a bit stressed, because she and Alisson were themselves packing up to leave for Arizona the next morning. As she ran to answer Stefan's call, she was greeted with the stench of dog poop…apparently someone had been feeding the dog table scraps again…and Mom wasn't even home to clean it up.

These faxes tell part of the continuing saga of that day. The girls also called approximately six times in this one-hour period.

FAX #1

Dear Mom,

There is a rat literally half the size of Marywether [the cat]. It's half alive and Marywether is playing with it because we locked her in (it's in Olivia's room), and it pooped all over, so much that it's lying in it and squishing it into the carpet.

Please call and HELP US as soon as you get this fax!!!!

We love you,

Alisson

Dear Mom —

We're not in total panic, but almost. Just kidding!

Love,

Olivia

The Totaled Woman

FAX #2

Dear Mom,

We got him outside by a bag. Olivia was going to smash it with a crutch, but then I realized that it was a chipmunk that Marywether brought inside. So, I brought it outside (in a bag) and put her near the creek. I felt SOOOOOOOOOOOOOOO sorry for her because she was half-dead and shivery on the wet ground outside because it's raining. I love you!

Love,

Alisson

From Olivia —

Do rats have naked tails? Because it had lots of fur and fur on its tail and it had stripes, sort of. Maybe it was a chipmunk? Exciting!!

But we (mainly Alisson) saved the day! We're so BRAVE!

My parents just sat dumbfounded as the phone calls and faxes tumbled in. I don't have the nerve to tell them that this is just life on a daily basis at our house.

—— Lively Locomotion ——

"Mom, did you know that Mr. Krebs can run?" Five breathless kids charged into the kitchen. Mr. Krebs was our cranky 75-year-old neighbor.

"Why on earth is he running?" I asked.

"Oh, that's the best part!" Nathan blurted out, "Mrs. Krebs is chasing him with the garden hose!"

"Yeah!" Ingrid burst in, "Mrs. Krebs can run too!"

This was too good to miss. The kids and I sneaked onto our back porch to watch. Mrs. Krebs stood defiantly in their back yard, brandishing the hose at her husband, who stood belligerently halfway across the yard. If it hadn't been so sad, it would have been funny.

In all the years they lived next to us, I don't think we ever saw them enjoying themselves, or each other. We prayed for them every night. Those prayers didn't seem to help their situation, but they helped us live next door to them. You see, they not only didn't like each other, they exhibited a loathing for us as well.

The Krebs' helped us all develop a good sense of humor, and an active prayer life. Only now that the kids are grown can I begin to perceive the gift God gave us in our miserable neighbors.

—— Believe It Or Not ——

I made a trip to the grocery store earlier this week to buy a large quantity of victuals for the masses. Upon my return, I requested some assistance with the disposal of the groceries that needed to go in the downstairs refrigerator or the freezer. Ten-year-old Stefan was assigned this task; Olivia took care of the paper goods and folding the grocery bags.

The next night, I trotted downstairs to fetch a bag of beans to go with the dinner. I opened the big freezer, and right there on top were two dozen very frozen eggs! I tried to speak kindly as I asked Stefan if he thought eggs usually were kept in the freezer. "Alisson [age five] told me to put them there," was his answer. I set them in the garbage, and went on with dinner preparations.

Suddenly, Stefan rounded the corner with Olivia and Nathan close behind. They had just read in *Ripley's Believe It or Not* that frozen eggs bounce! Off they ran to the garage with a dozen frozen eggs.

Shattered egg shells are difficult to sweep up, as they found out…I think they'll peel the critters next time they try it.

— A Big Move —

When we moved from Rochester, Minnesota to Hershey, Pennsylvania, little Nathan had just turned three. As diligent parents, we had been coaching our two little ones about this move; trying to tell them all the positives and how exciting it would be to be in a new place. Hershey seemed like such a wonderful place to Nathan, who was old enough to understand more than little Ingrid; I mean, the home of chocolate bars! It even smelled like chocolate! As we pulled into the parking spot in front of our new home – a townhouse within walking distance of the medical center – we caught sight of our new neighbor…an athletic-looking black man.

We juggled ourselves, our luggage and the kids into our new home, and settled down on the empty carpeted floor to await the moving van.

Just then there was a knock on the door. As we opened it, a big smile greeted us and we shook hands with our new neighbor, Joe. Nathan was dumbfounded as he stood looking at the first black person he had ever seen (Minnesota is all Scandinavians!). Actually, Nathan was thrilled! He shook Joe's hand and asked in reverent wonder, "Are you the Hershey Man?"

—— Hyacinths to Feed the Soul ——

Our life goes on apace…this morning, for example…all of the kids were bickering (too tired after a late basketball game at school). I went to let the barking dog in, and she ran off into the woods with me in hot pursuit (did I mention the pouring rain?). It's amazing that an overweight middle-aged dog can run so much faster than a lean middle-aged woman.

As we assembled in the car for the ride to school, the car spluttered and died after Johannes had backed out of the garage. We all piled out of the car, and scrambled quickly into the van (did I mention the persistent rain?) while Daddy nursed the lurching, dying car back into the garage. All this before 8:00 a.m.….sigh.

AAA towed the car to the mechanic, so we're down to one vehicle… how convenient!

The kids are still at school, baby Alisson is asleep, the second load of white things is in the washer, six loads of wash are folded and put away, the chili is made for dinner with fresh homemade bread to go with it. I am ignoring the dishwasher filled with clean dishes, the sink filled with dirty dishes, the Christmas tree that needs to be taken down, the nativity scene, the Christmas village, and candles…much done, much to do…a perfect time for a cup of hot spiced tea.

—— It Can't Get Any Worse Than This! ——

This is an actual letter from camp…(If you don't believe me, I have the hand-written one to prove it!):

Dear Mommy,

I can't stand it. I miss you to [sic] much. I keep bursting out in tears in front of everyone. It's so embarrassing. I have to come home. PLEASE pick me up EXTRA, EXTRA, EXTRA EARLY PLEASE!

We have to stay up until 10:30, then read till 11:00. It is too LATE for me. I hate it here come pick me up SOON, SOON, SOON, SOON. It is no fun in the creek, because I don't have my water shoes. And I'm too homesick to eat. I have not eaten in days. I never have breakfast or dinner, and I only nibble something at lunch. Everything else I can't do, because I can't run or I'll get a cramp. All we do is running here. I get nightmares in the middle of the night and wake everybody up. And I cry day and night, because I miss you. But I hide it, until I burst out in tears. Like right now, I'm crying, I just can't help it. Now that you see how bad camp is, PLEASE! PICK ME UP EARLY!!!!!

I could never explain how much I love you.

Love and hugs & kisses,

Believe it or not, I have six such letters — all written in that seven-day period.

— Out of Sight, So It Seemed —

The last thing I said to the kids when they started to clean up the kitchen after dinner was, "Do not feed the dog any table scraps; if you do, she will poop all over, and you'll be the one to clean it up."

Several innocent faces smiled at me, as if to say, "I'd never think of it, Mom!" Right…

The next morning, as I hurried around fixing lunches, breakfast, and feeding the animals, I was overwhelmed by the stench coming from the lower level! Cursory investigation showed that Bandit had, indeed, pooped all over the carpet in the lower living room. As I grabbed my school bag, lunch and coffee, I stopped by the room of the delinquent dog feeder (it was obvious which kid did it), and told him that he would have to have that mess cleaned up before he left for school. Wonderful start to a day of teaching!

The carpet was spotless when I got home from school! The strange thing was, the new Hoover vacuum cleaner was sitting on the front porch. It seems that the dog feeder was not really into cleaning up disgusting poop as a start to his day, so he just vacuumed up the semi-liquid material, and left it, still in the vacuum, on the front porch. After all, out of sight, out of mind, right?

I wonder if that's how I handle the tasks the Lord gives me. I don't want to fix what I've messed up; I just want to forget about it, and let someone else take care of the mess.

─── Dependent Independence ───

While he is attending the local community college, Stefan has moved into his own apartment with a buddy from high school. It is so nice to have him be independent, and yet nearby...I think. While we are all away during the school day, the egg bandito slinks home, scrambles up a half-dozen eggs, drinks all the orange juice, grabs some cookies, and is gone without a trace.

Yesterday, he came home and mowed the lawn (it pays $15). After I paid him and he was headed to his car, I noticed that he had (1) the wastebasket from my sewing room, (2) several tubs of margarine (hidden in the wastebasket), (3) a special nightlight that he had just bought as a present for Alisson, and (4) the 3-tiered wooden lazy Susan that my parents gave me years ago to use at Christmastime. I let him keep the margarine.

Today he came home about 4:00 p.m. with his laundry, and wondered if "we" could get it done before work at 5:00. He asked me if I could just fold the clothes (when I get them washed, that is), and set them in the back seat of his car; he'll leave the door open for me. How thoughtful!

As he left for work with his clean laundry, I noticed that he had the Electrolux under his arm! I wonder if I should take him the wand that goes with it. Somehow, I enjoy the thought of his vacuuming with just the nozzle.

I wonder if I approach being part of God's family like that. I want the independence to be able to be "on my own," but would like the convenience of getting whatever I might need from "home," no strings attached. We see the humor here on earth; we realize the presumption when viewed with a heavenly perspective.

The Totaled Woman

—— What Kind of a Bird Are You? ——

"Ingrid, the time has come…go downstairs and clean your room!"

"Aw, Mom! I want to go out with the other kids and play!"

But I was firm, and down the stairs she went to face the world's messiest bedroom. No wonder she didn't want to clean it; it was almost beyond human intervention!

"Mom!" She was back upstairs already - gesticulating wildly, gasping, eyes wide. "Mom!" - hands waving in the air hysterically, "There's an owl in my room!"

This was the last straw; I was sick and tired of her procrastinating. I would tolerate no more excuses. "Ingrid, as messy as that room is, you are probably seeing one of your stuffed animals that has fallen to an unaccustomed place. Now get down there and clean that room!"

Now, several of our children fall into the classic "strong-willed" category, but not Ingrid…frustrated at times, emotional on occasion, but not the type to look me in the eye and say, "No way!"

"You can kill me if you want, but I'm not going back down there!" said our mild-tempered daughter.

We were at an impasse, until older brother Nathan stepped gallantly into the gap. "I'll go downstairs with her, Mom," he said, eyeing his not-very-much-younger sister condescendingly. "Come on, Ingrid."

At last, she was about to make some order out of the chaos below. But here they both came galloping up the stairs; neither one speaking, both waving their arms insanely. Nathan was gasping as if he had just emerged from beneath the water, and spluttered incoherently, "There IS an owl in her room, Mom! Honest!"

Oh darn. Now I was going to have to leave the mess in the kitchen and deal with these kids, who obviously had no grasp on reality…Down the stairs we went; Nathan and Ingrid cowering behind me, pushing me forward to meet "the owl."

I walked into Ingrid's bedroom and looked around cursorily. "There is nothing here, kids," I chuckled…And then I looked up…

On the top of one of the opened louvered closet doors sat the biggest horned owl I have ever seen. Now it was my turn to gasp. He was over a foot tall, with talons that extended several inches down the door. He sat imperiously, his yellow eyes piercing through me as if to say, "You idiot! What are you staring at? Haven't you ever seen an owl before?"

I did what any thinking wife and mother would do at such a time: I ran to the phone and called Johannes; husbands always know the right thing to do, right? I explained the situation as rationally as I could. After a lengthy pause, he said, "Well, I actually have a lot of unfinished things here at the hospital, so I can't come home quite yet…why don't you just take Olivia's butterfly net and catch him, then you can let him loose out the front door." I could hardly blame him for not really believing me…a butterfly net? Whom were we kidding? That fellow on the closet door was no butterfly! Realizing I was not so easily placated he said, "Call the SPCA, I'm sure they deal with these things all the time."

So, I called the SPCA. "An owl, you say?" the voice on the line questioned cautiously. "And where did you say it is?" This fellow obviously thought I had lost my marbles. Well, he was in good company, that's what my husband thought too. The SPCA man finally agreed to send someone out to "assess the situation." They must have looked about and found the most expendable youngster in their employ, and said, "Would you go check out this weirdo?"

The young woman arrived. Her condescending look of pity told the story: she had been sent to pacify insanity. Triumphantly, the kids and I escorted her down the stairs to the bedroom. The now-familiar gasp reached our ears. She bolted from the room with a look of utter shock.

But two heads were better than one, and we decided to open the windows and just shoo him out! Now why hadn't I thought of that? So, we discussed who would do what, and decided that she would open the windows – which were bolted shut and had to be unbolted with a special tool – and I would "shoo him out." By this time, it was approaching dusk, and we were certain of success, because everyone knows that owls prefer the darkness to the light. The windows were wide open, and I looked at our feathered friend and waved my hands mildly and said, "Shoo."

Owl - eyes never blinking or moving - looked at me as if to say, "What is your problem?" He had no intention of going anywhere! I sent the kids to find the broom. Surely, this would do the trick. Holding the broom end and proffering the handle, I approached Owl and again said "shoo" while prodding toward him with the broom handle. As if in slow motion, he spread his wings (span of over three feet!), grabbed hold of the broom handle with his immense talons, and again folded his wings. Of course, once he folded those wings, he was a dead weight on the broom. He was so heavy that I could not possibly hold him! Thankfully, there was a bureau right below the handle. With all my might, I slowed the descent of the broom and owl so that he landed rather gently on Ingrid's dresser, within two feet of me. We were now eyeball to eyeball. He was still grasping the broom handle, and I had neither strength nor leverage to remove it. We had come to a stalemate.

The Totaled Woman

The girl from the SPCA felt she had done all she could to help, and left hurriedly. Chicken.

It was now approaching dinner time. I, of course, had no plans for an evening meal. Our lives had been so wrapped up in Owl, that we had considered nothing else for several hours. Just then, I heard the kids squeal and run to the front door. I am sure Johannes thought the owl was long gone, and that it was safe to come home. If only he had come when I called him! He had the perfect idea!

He and Nathan took a bed sheet, holding it vertically to make a sort of fake wall behind Owl. Slowly, they moved toward the window holding the portable "wall". Owl first jumped from the dresser to the floor, then hopped across the floor, finally spreading his wings and disappearing out the window.

It was over. Only after he was gone did the kids and I stop to inquire just how our visitor had found his way into Ingrid's bedroom. We just laughed when we finally looked with eyes that were able to focus on more than the crisis. He had fallen down the chimney! That intelligent bird with the never-blinking yellow eyes who looked down on us in apparent pity, had sat down in the middle of the chimney, plummeted down the sooty shaft, staggered through the living room depositing black smudges every step of the way, and finally flown to apparent safety on the door of Ingrid's closet.

You know, Owl was a fake. Oh no, he was a real owl! But he was pretending to be something he wasn't. He really was just lost and confused; even though he projected wisdom and intelligence. The funny part is that we intelligent human beings believed him, because we were too wrapped up in the crisis to consider. Hmm, Lord, what is it You are saying in all this?

⸺ A Day in the Life... ⸺

As I entered the grocery-store parking lot, my cell phone rang...

"Hi Mom! I want to tell you about the mouse in my kitchen."

I hate mice! I don't really want to know!

"Oh, do you have a mouse in your kitchen?"

"Not anymore! I found him in the bottom of my garbage can; so I threw him, can and all out the door. You should have seen him, Mom, he was jumping up and down on the side of the can."

Ewwwww, I don't want to know!

"Well, I'm glad you were able to get rid of him."

"Yeah, me too! Well, I'll talk with you later. Bye!"

"Hello, Mom, could you do me a favor?"

No problem! I'm just here at home doing my toenails...a woman of leisure...

I have returned the microphones we rented from the sound store for the church Easter program yesterday, gone by the church and picked up all the fake trees and bushes we borrowed from a neighboring church, dropped off the stools a church family lent us for the play, and made a quick jaunt into the grocery store. The piano tuner won't be here for an hour...

"Sure! What do you need?"

"I need to know how to cite different types of internet sources; and I have to turn this paper in by this afternoon! Could you just email me the information right away?"

"No problem!" *Hmmm, where in the world did I put that research-paper curriculum?*

The Totaled Woman

"Hey Mom! Would you mind proof-reading my latest research paper on soccer and South African politics? I just emailed it to you; and I don't need it until tomorrow morning. Thanks!"

"Sure, no problem!"

Oh my gosh, it is 30 pages long! I haven't finished my Bible-study lesson for tomorrow morning, nor have I practiced the songs we are singing. Oh well, the pianist can 'wing it', right?

"Mother dear, I need help! I can't download this PDF file for my outline for linguistics; could you give it a try? I'll instant-message you the website right now."

Oh no! I just clicked the wrong button and erased her IM with the website on it!

"Mom! Where in the Bible is the phrase, 'He who lives by the sword dies by the sword.'? Please email me soon; I need to include it in my paper! Thanks!"

Google is faster than Strong's Concordance. Did you know that quote is in three of the four gospels?

It is almost time to start dinner, but I think I'll just pour out a few m&m's to help get me through the rest of the afternoon...

I poured half a bag of m&m's into the puppy's dog dish, which was on the counter next to the dish I meant to use.

—— ...Oft Go Astray ——

"Okay, now I've written out all the instructions for you," I smiled confidently as I prepared to leave for work and my husband prepared to leave for class. Such confidence was grounded on a faulty premise, which led to... well, let me just explain:

We were going to have a lamb roast for dinner, which Johannes needed to pop in the oven when he got home from class at the medical center. We had not been married long, and I had only a partial understanding of the scientific mind. I was so proud of myself! I placed the roast in the roasting pan in the fridge. I wrote instructions for every step: "1. remove roast from refrigerator, 2. remove plastic wrap from roast, 3. turn oven to bake at 325, 4. put roast in the oven (top rack), 5. shut oven door."

As I entered the house after work, the roast smelled wonderful. I was so pleased...but Johannes was very upset. "Don't you know," he snapped, "that you have to put it in a pan before you put it in the oven? It went all over the oven the way you told me to do it!" Alas, I had neglected to tell him to remove the pan from the refrigerator, and to place the unwrapped meat in it before putting it in the oven. In science, one must be very precise. It took hours to clean the oven, but I learned my lesson. Precision in thinking and giving directions are a must!

—— ...Still Go Astray ——

We have now been married 37 years; Johannes is a world-renowned researcher and professor of medicine. I recently left his lunch in the microwave for him to heat when he got home. I set the time for 90 seconds, and left this note: "Simply push start (90 seconds) and enjoy your chili."

This time, I gave him too much information! He pushed "90" into the timer making the time "9090" and turned it on, totally forgetting it until that one cup of chili (covered with a plastic margarine top) had cooked on "high" for an hour. The stench of melted plastic was overpowering! Of course, there was nothing left of the chili, it had turned to ash long ago.

—— Reciprocity ——

In all fairness, I must relate this one last tale. I had made arrangements for us to meet out-of-town friends in Washington, D.C. We drove the 2 hours on that Saturday, caught the metro to Chevy Chase on the far side of Washington, and arrived at their hotel in a timely fashion…they weren't there.

I looked at Johannes and said, "Is this the 12th?"

"No," he responded, "It is the 11th, why?"

"Oh nothing." I tried to appear unconcerned, "It's just that I have the wrong day. We are supposed to meet them tomorrow."

We never did get to see our friends. When they returned from their outing to the national zoo, they called us – so concerned that they had missed us, even though it was my mistake. Our friend said, "Was Johannes very upset with you?"

Not only was he not upset, he was the happiest man alive! For once, I had made the pre-occupied error. Gentleman that he is, he has never brought it up again. He is just happy to know that such things happen to multi-tasking English teachers as well as absent-minded scientists.

Moo

We were all a little crotchety this morning. We live in a cul de sac, and a car across the circle from us has a defective alarm system. Many a time during the day, we are treated to unattended honking. I am fighting the opinion that the people who own the car also have a few defects, but I'm afraid I'm losing the battle.

The horn first blasted its way into our consciousness at 2:00 a.m., and continued its rhythmic honking for five to ten minutes. At 6:00, it set off again...and again at 6:30. Somehow we resented this on Memorial Day even more than a regular work day, when we are up at 6:00 anyway.

The folks across the way finally came outside about 10:30 to enjoy the holiday. Apparently, they could sleep in. I sauntered across the street and in my most civil manner asked them if they knew that their car had awakened the neighborhood numerous times. The man of the house just looked at me with a bovine expression of unconcern; I actually thought he might moo... His wife was much more helpful; she explained that the wind often made the alarm go off. And she smiled as if that answered the question and the problem. Mustering all his energy, the husband said, "Well, maybe we ought to disconnect the alarm sometime."

I have been pondering both their uncon- cern and my irritation. Lord, I'd rather blame the wind, or just gaze vacantly when You are plainly speaking to me about something that I need to work on in my life. I might even know what I should do about it, but I'd really rather smile unconcernedly and go on about my own business. I wonder how irritated the Lord gets with me, when I smile and moo at Him.

—— A Happy Cat ——

If this morning's trauma were in a soap opera, you would turn it off and say, "Oh my gosh, that is so dumb! That would never happen!" mmhhmm

It's a calm sunny morning, so I decided to open the umbrella on the back porch table, which I did. As I walked back inside, I heard the strangest "cheep, cheep" noise. The cheeping followed me inside, and I realized it was coming from my own head! I performed some convulsive head-whirling maneuver, and – plop – a brown animal about the size of a giant bullfrog fell to the ground. Wings unfolded from the cheeping brown mass, as I recoiled in disbelief and revulsion. A bat had obviously been asleep in the folded-up umbrella.

I have no idea how I got the thing out the door. Surely I didn't pick it up…did I? Bilbo is the happiest cat on earth right now. He was just resting in the corner of the porch when this cheeping morning delicacy appeared from nowhere! He picked it up, and strolled off into the yard.

I have washed my hair. I'm sure there will be a time I'll find this humorous…but not right now.

—— In the Dog House ——

I decided to skip the gym this morning...after all, I am still moving things around in the laundry room to accommodate the puppy...you see, this morning about 4:30, I heard thumping in the laundry room (where the dogs are confined at night), but thought Caspian was just playing with his rag 'bone'. Heh, heh...nope...he was playing with the plastic bottles of tempera paint, specifically, the black. By the time I got up at 6:00, he had shredded the contents of the recycle newspaper bin and opened and liberally distributed the black paint. He greeted me with a big black smile and smudgy black paws. Of course, the tile floor was a mass of black footprints.

So, I'm rearranging the laundry room this morning...since I've already washed the puppy and the floor...and all this before 7:00 a.m.! I just love those people who ask me how I'm dealing with the "empty nest!" At least when the nest was full of kids, I could get them to clean it up.

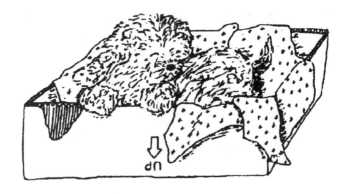

The Totaled Woman

—— Difficult People ——

Roy took a daily walk, always strolling with his head down, hands clasped behind his back. Never would he smile, or look up – even when we said, "Hello." Our dog knew an enemy when she saw one, and always barked at him. Since he never looked up, he never saw her coming toward him until she was right next to him…the dog barked wildly, and Roy swore and spit at her. This happened every day for all the years they lived next to us.

Roy planted 50 rosebushes, telling our children that they would grow to be five feet high, and then their balls could not get into his yard. Every day during the spring and summer he would go out to tend those bushes, watering, trimming, cultivating and muttering. By the next spring, it was obvious they all had died. We tried not to smirk, at least not where he could see us.

After we had put up our fence, Roy planted giant pyracantha bushes. They flourished, as did his malice, and grew to be about eight feet high. The thorns were not to be believed or touched! Nathan fondly called them the "Sleeping Beauty Bushes," and believe me, it would have taken a magic sword to demolish them. One day, I realized that we would have to trim the huge bowers that were encroaching upon our yard and flower garden. Nathan and I approached the bushes armed with heavy gloves and pruning shears. It was a perilous task, but we were able to beat them back somewhat. When we moved away some years later, the bushes were still growing and spreading.

Dear Lord, help us to show Your love regardless of the difficult people around us, and please help us to not be difficult ourselves!

—— Unfounded Confidence ——

Olivia was 18 months old. Since she was our third child, I felt fairly confident in my mothering skills, discipline, and such...

Ingrid and Nathan were at preschool, so Olivia and I took a walk around the neighborhood. As we approached the street corner, I said to Olivia, "Now, you must hold Mommy's hand, because cars are dangerous."

Sweet little thing looked up at me with those innocent brown eyes and blonde hair... "No."

Surely, she just hadn't heard me, so I tried again. "Hold my hand while we cross the road, Olivia."

"No."

Well, this was child number three, and I knew I had to win. I took hold of her hand and started across the road. Halfway across, Olivia performed what I call the 'jelly-leg maneuver', sitting right down in the middle of the road. I picked her up, walked back to the sidewalk, set her down and said, "You hold my hand!"

"No."

Oh darn! Now what do I do? Well, I must win this battle; so I gave her a smart pat on her double diaper and said again, "You hold my hand!"

"No."

My next "pat" reached below the diaper to the uncovered upper leg. Then I said, "Now, Olivia, hold my hand!" She did! And we crossed the road without further incident. I immediately let go of her hand when we reached the other side. Breathing a sigh of relief, I was so thankful that I had won that battle.

In the very midst of such thoughts, Olivia ran up behind me and smacked me on the bottom! As I wheeled about in utter amazement, she looked up at me, pointed her chubby little finger, and said, "You hold my hand!"

Actually, I think I lost

—— Fatal ——

Johannes was just sitting down to work (as if he hasn't already done a day's worth before arriving home), and I was pointing out a few things… mail, questions about friends who were coming to spend a week with us while they visited the clinic, his need for a haircut, reminding him to drink his freshly brewed coffee…

He was trying to enjoy my ministrations, and said (somewhat wearily, I thought), "What would I do without you?"

I responded airily, "Oh, you'd probably get more work done, but the rest of your life would be a bit dull."

As I headed to the back room, I heard a contemplative voice mutter, "More like fatal."

Ah yes, Lord! That is how our lives would be without You – fatal!

—— The Rumors of My Death... ——

It was Saturday, and Stefan's soccer dinner was at 5:00, to celebrate the end of a successful season. Johannes had to go by the hospital before that, so we decided to just meet there; I would bring the kids, he would bring himself...what could be more straightforward and easy?

At 5:30, Johannes was still not there...6 o'clock came and went...by 6:30, the dinner and awards were about over, and I was positively worried. On the way home, I stopped by the doughnut shop where 14-year-old Ingrid was working, and asked her if she had seen her dad. No, he hadn't come by.

We drove home, and I tried calling his office at the hospital...no answer. His cell phone was turned off...again. We didn't have an answering machine, so there was no message. Now, worrying is one of the things I do best, and by this point, I had convinced myself that something terrible had happened. I mean, he was complaining of feeling poorly. Maybe he was at the hospital and had had a heart attack, or been mugged in the elevator, or...........oh the possibilities were endless to the fertile mind.

Leaving the children in Nathan's care, I took off to scour the hospital, stopping at the information desk, and asking for the campus police to escort me to his office. I mean, I wasn't ready to find his body alone! We searched the couple of rooms – his office and lab – at which point, the policeman suggested that I look in the bathroom. I told him that if Dr. Veldhuis were in the bathroom, he would be either dead or unconscious, so how about if he went in to check. He did, and no one was there.

At this point, the policeman said he would contact the University security chief, and put out a bulletin for a missing person; he left me in Johannes' office to go talk with his chief and get things rolling. I now called Johannes'

The Totaled Woman

colleagues, to ask if they had heard from him. No one had, but one of them offered to come help me look for him.

By now, it was 8:30, and it occurred to me that I should check in with the kids, since they too had been worried sick. I stopped by the doughnut shop, and Ingrid came sprinting out to tell me that Olivia had just called to say that Dad was alive and safe, and on his way home from Richmond! He had finally turned on his cell phone to call home. Olivia had answered, and upon hearing her dad, burst into tears. "Oh my goodness, Dad, are you okay?"

His answer was a surprised, "Why wouldn't I be okay?" Johannes had driven the 60 miles to Richmond to get a surprise for the family – a new video camera.

It was a surprise all right.

The next day, he was mortified to find that his disappearance was pretty much common knowledge all over the medical center. When he got home from work, this hand-written note was waiting for him on his dresser:

Dad,

Please report to your room promptly without dinner. I will talk to you then, after you hand over your keys for a week. (In other words, you're grounded and fined $20!)

Nathan

P.S. You're in trouble!

—— Up In Smoke ——

Johannes had been on a trip, and we expected him home in the early evening. Stefan wanted to do something special for his arrival, and hit upon a novel plan…I occasionally peeked out the window as he made elaborate preparations, building something that looked like a funeral pyre in the middle of the driveway. He assembled several cardboard boxes, piling them to make a table-like arrangement. He then sprinted over to the neighbor-boys' house, coming back with something that looked a bit like birthday candles, which he set in a paper cup on top of the boxes.

Of course, I had other things to do besides watch my 12-year-old, so I worked around in the kitchen for a few minutes, looking out the window just in time to see giant flames leaping from Stefan's "funeral pyre" as if it were a suttee! Stefan, shoes also aflame, was racing across the yard, jumping and yelling. This was my call to action! I flew out the front door and tackled my son as he sprinted by, rolling over and over in the grass until we had smothered the flames on his shoes. We then sat there in the grass and watched the cardboard boxes burn to the ground.

What in the world had he been doing? The answer, Stefan told me, was simple…He had some firecrackers (illegal in the state of Virginia) that his friends had given him, and he wanted to make sure they would ignite as his dad drove in the driveway. So he took a couple of them to try. But just to make sure, he found the fire-starter for the grill, and poured it all over, which accidentally included his shoes.

We never really forgot that day, since the driveway fire was hot enough to melt the asphalt, leaving a smooth indentation where the boxes had been. The firecrackers never did ignite.

I wonder how often I play with 'fire', and never realize the danger. Dear Lord, save me from my own foolishness masquerading as intelligent thought!

—— Counting to Four ——

Nathan's soccer match was running late, and Ingrid's gymnastics class was about to begin - all the way across town. Fortunately, we had foreseen that this might happen, and drove two cars. Nathan was guarding the goal, Stefan and Olivia were playing happily in the stones nearby, Johannes was watching the game; I was quite pregnant with Alisson. All were accounted for, so I reminded Johannes that he had three children to bring home...Ingrid and I left for gymnastics.

By the time Johannes' car pulled into the driveway, I was already home. He and Nathan walked into the foyer and shut the door. "Where are the little ones?" I asked.

"Well, I suppose they are taking their naps by now," Johannes responded confidently.

There are some stories that never really are funny, and this one is in that category. All mothers have their worries...mine had always been that someone might take our children. And now, two little blond-haired tots were alone on a playing field in one of the worst sections of Charlottesville.

Driving to the field was one of the longest trips of my life. Of course, the field was bare...not a person in sight. I ran about that empty field calling their names to no avail. There was a pool at the school next to the field, and I inquired if anyone had seen two little blond children. No, no one had seen them.

I went back to the car and called home. Stefan answered the phone! It seems that the Carmichaels had forgotten their water dish for their new puppy they brought to the field, and came back to retrieve it. The Carmichaels lived in our neighborhood, and it was the only time they ever brought their dog to a game. They found Olivia and Stefan standing bewildered near the parking lot, and brought them home.

After a good cry, I drove home. Poor Johannes...I didn't speak to him all day, but it wasn't because I was angry...I just didn't want to cry in front of the children or him. At every game until the end of the season, the other parents asked us before we left the field, "Have you counted to four?"

The children were unaware of the danger. They thought Daddy was just playing a game, as they watched him drive off. Lord, help us to know that You never leave us or forget us even for a moment.

—— Shoelace ——

Johannes cemented up the hole, mostly to placate his wife who suffers from a phobia toward naked-tailed creatures. He tried to assure me that we did not have a rat in the house…a little mouse perhaps, but certainly nothing of the proportions my active imagination had conjured up. After two weeks of loud banging in my cupboards at night, and other disgusting evidences of a large rodent, I put out rat poison, which was gobbled up with great gusto by something (hopefully not the cat!).

It's been two months since then, and we've had no more evidence of the critter (and the cat is still alive). Today, I decided it was time to redo the laundry room: set the boots in a cupboard, vacuum, and generally clean up in there. There certainly did seem to be a huge pile of dust, and even an old long shoelace behind those boots…I tried to pick up the 'shoelace', however, it was attached to the 'dust' on the floor…

When Nathan gets home from soccer tonight, I am going to ask him to kindly remove the nonexistent rat; but for now, I am having a little trouble getting up the nerve to finish the wash. The funny thing is, I'd been co-existing with a dead rat for two months or more, and never worried – until I found out it was there, and dead.

Maybe we'll hide it away in the garage until Johannes gets home from Canada. I'm sure he'd enjoy seeing it, don't you think?

The Totaled Woman

—— Holding Hands ——

Alisson was four years old. She and I were at what is known as 'the Corner' at the University of Virginia, crossing that very dangerous intersection to meet Daddy for a doughnut.

As we neared the sidewalk, Alisson suddenly let go of my hand and turned back into the road to retrieve her barrette, which she had dropped. Just as she did this, a car careened around the corner, heading straight for her. Since she was little to begin with, when she bent down to pick up her barrette, the driver couldn't see her at all. Now, I have never been a screamer, but there is a first time for all things…and this was the time to scream. I did, and the driver slammed on his brakes, barely missing our youngest child.

I held Alisson's hand until we were safely in the doughnut shop. She looked up at me with those adorable brown eyes, and said, "Mommy, I'm worried about you."

I picked her up and hugged her, saying, "Alisson, don't ever let go of Mommy's hand in the road! We can get a new barrette, but I can't get a new Alisson!"

With four-year-old wisdom she answered, "Uh huh, Mommy! Jesus could make a new me!" She was right, of course. But her pointing us to the Savior caused me to realize the basic problem that day – I was not really holding her hand, she was holding mine. Believe me, from then on I held her so that she could not let go of me without my allowing it.

Thank you, Lord, that I cannot escape your grasp.

—— Luftmensch ——

Olivia had just turned sixteen, and was driving her dad to Roanoke where he was collaborating with another scientist/physician. They had been on the road for about an hour – Olivia at the wheel, Johannes working on his papers – when the gas-gauge light (fondly known as the idiot light) came on and beeped a reminder periodically. They mentioned how they should stop and fill up, and at the next exit, they pulled into a gas station, parked, went inside, bought peanuts and snacks, got back in the car and back on the highway…

There is a wonderful German word that applies to this story – *Luftmensch: Luft* means 'air', *Mensch* means 'person'; In this case, the *Mensches* were fairly high in the atmosphere. We do have a few *Lufties* in our family…

Olivia set the cruise control, and started up a huge hill, when the car began to lurch. She told her father that she thought there was something wrong with the cruise control. Johannes thought about it for awhile, looked at the gauge, and said, "It's out of gas! Since you are driving, Olivia, you really ought to check the gas gauge!"

They pulled off to the side of the road as the car spluttered to a stop. Ahead they saw a sign advertising a gas station at the next exit, so they decided to hitchhike there. Eventually, two 18-wheelers pulled over…Olivia got in one, her father got in the other. As the trucks re-entered the highway, it occurred to Johannes that perhaps this was not such a good idea – sending his beautiful 16-year-old daughter off alone with a strange man.

They were a little late for Johannes' appointment in Roanoke, but at least they both lived to tell the story.

——— You're Where? ———

When we moved halfway across the country, we asked Stefan and his friend, LJ, if they would be willing to drive Johannes' car with the two dogs to our new home. We suggested they take two days for the drive, and that they spend a night at a hotel along the way. Since we would be staying in a hotel for a few days before we could move into our new house, they were to arrive three days after we did, and come to the new house, which would be ready and waiting by then. We were pretty firm about their not trying to drive it all at one stretch, and made sure they had enough money for meals and a hotel.

That was the plan...reality was a different matter...

We had been at the Marriott two days, and were planning to meet the moving van the following morning. At 3:00 a.m., the phone rang in our room..."Hey Mom, we're here! What should we do with the dogs?"

We were not amused. I put on my slippers, found my way to the elevator, and appeared – rather miffed – at the front desk in my pajamas. There was Stefan. LJ was still in the car with the dogs. Now the Marriott Inn does not normally accommodate dogs from out of town, but they were kind enough to allow the boys (and dogs) a room on the smoking floor. I staggered back to our room about 3:30 a.m., leaving the boys to figure out how to get the dogs into the elevator and such.

As we ate breakfast the next morning (the dogs were back in the car), the whole sordid tale came out. The trip had been fairly uneventful, until the fellows were driving around Chicago. When they stopped for gas, they left the windows open for the dogs to have some air...bad idea...both dogs leaped from the car and headed off across the expressway at a gallop. LJ ran into the expressway after one, Stefan did the same for the other. Miraculously, both boys and dogs survived unscathed.

Such stories, even in retrospect, give a mother gray hair...

—— Sex at Six? ——

"Mommy, what is sex?"

We had just arrived home from school, and my second-grader looked at me for the answer to his question. Nathan has always been a precocious little boy, and I wondered if this was a normal question for one so young. Since he was our first, I had no idea such a question could come so early...and I was not prepared!

"Well, Nathan," I stammered, and I started on this big explanation about mommies and daddies, cats having kittens, the birds and the bees...I was sinking fast and praying earnestly for wisdom and the right words.

Finally, I asked him what made him ask about sex; to which he responded nonchalantly, "Oh, well, I was trying to fill out this form for the new school year, and it says, 'Sex'...so, what should I put there? About mommies and daddies, or about the cats? There is only a little space, you know."

—— Out of the Mouths of Babes ——

We were on our way to the hippy store. Actually, it was the health-food store, but we called it the hippy store because they sold all sorts of "Mother Earth" items and magazines, and the clerks had a pacific air about them as if they had been smoking something other than cigarettes. In short, it reminded us of the hippies of the '60s...love and peace, man...

As we entered the store, Nathan, who was about 12, noticed a picture of a guru on the wall — robes, beard and all. "Hey Mom!" he shouted, "There he is! There's the hypocrite!"

It was then I realized that Nathan didn't really know what a hippy was, and thought it was short for 'hypocrite'.

We quickly made our choices from the bins of flour, yeast and spices, paid for our items and escaped as quickly as possible. Of course, we were from then on pegged as the enemy. Whenever I entered the store, all friendliness vanished. They didn't mind having our business, but they showed their disdain.

I suppose I could have been upset with Nathan, but I wasn't. What he said was nearer the truth than I cared to admit, at least while we were in the store. Our preteen was not being judgmental; he was saying truth as he saw it, without the reservation that comes with age and maturity.

Sometimes I think age and maturity rob us of the ability to see things as they really are, and the forthrightness to speak when perhaps we should.

—— The Dynamic Duo ——

It is suffocatingly hot in Virginia in the summertime. We needed to shave our husky's thick long fur for her to survive the 90-degree temperatures. When I called the groomer, she informed me that after the last attempt to clip Bandit, she would no longer do it. Bandit is a lovable but neurotic dog, I must admit, and biting the hand that grooms you is not the way to win friends.

So, it was up to us. The veterinarian suggested giving her a valium to help calm her, and supplied us with a modest prescription of 12 pills, so we would have it on hand for future clippings. The dynamic duo of Stefan and LJ were the tonsorial experts in this case, and exuded great confidence in their abilities. I was thankful, because I really didn't want to tackle that job with a 60-pound pooch.

Now, Stefan has always been a bit compulsive, and figured that if one dose is good, a double dose is twice as good...By the time they were through clipping Bandit, they had given her 12 valium. Unfortunately, the medication made her more and more hyper instead of calming her down. So, the more they gave her, the worse it got.

She was the most pitiful-looking creature you can imagine by the time the ordeal was completed – three hours later. Not only was she drugged to the hilt, she was embarrassed at her new look. Totally dejected and exhausted, she hid under the porch for several days. A neighbor girl mistook Bandit for a deer, so deformed was she in her shorn state.

We never tried to clip her again. She had to just suffer with the heat. Poor Bandit was just ignorant of our trying to help her. She struggled against us because she couldn't understand the whole picture. She only knew about the clippers, not the end result.

I think that is how I am so many times. I look only at the life-trial I am experiencing, and not at the whole picture the Lord is painting in my life. Help me, Lord, to trust Your plan.

—— A Piece of Cake ——

Nathan was two, Ingrid was a baby. We had gone to the mall for a sanity break. Mothers of little ones need such breaks to communicate, even superficially, with persons over the age of two.

Actually, it was my 30th birthday, and I needed some cheering up. So, there we were at the children's clothing store, with the nice young couple who ran it and had a little play area at the back. As the kids played, and I chatted with the owners, an older woman wandered into the store, looked around for a few minutes, and then approached me. "Are you their grandmother?" she asked.

I was stunned. "Why would you think I was their grandmother?" I asked rather peevishly.

"Well, I thought only grandparents took time to hug the children," she replied.

I tried to find the positive side of what she was saying. I mean, after all, I did hug my children, and that was a positive thing, right? Finally, I realized that her comments were the most depressing thing I'd ever heard. Apparently I looked haggard enough to be mistaken for a woman twice my age. It was some consolation that the owners of the store took her to task, and told her she was way off base. But not much...

There was a bright side to this story...every other birthday since has been a piece of cake! As each decade rolls around, I think back to that day in the mall on my 30th birthday, and say to myself, "This is nothing compared to turning 30!"

—— Effective Squeeze ——

Daddy was out of town that Sunday morning, so after church we decided to splurge and go to lunch at the steakhouse. As we finished our meal, Nathan began playing with the little packages of mayonnaise, ketchup and mustard. First he and Stefan played soccer with them, trying to flick them into the other's 'goal' (actually their fingers held up to simulate the goal).

Lunch with a crew of five kids takes awhile to finish, and while I was busy with some of the younger kids, Nathan and Stefan decided to squeeze the packets to see how much squeezing it would take before they burst. I told the boys this was not a good idea, that they might squirt the contents all over, but of course, young boys will keep experimenting…

Nathan gave a particularly effective squeeze to his mustard packet, which sprang a leak…the mustard shot across our table to the neighboring table, where it landed on the shoulder of a gentleman's white sport coat. Nathan apologized to the man, and we offered to have his coat cleaned, but the gentleman kindly said it was all right, and that he didn't need to have the coat cleaned. Nathan was so relieved, and Stefan was so glad it was Nathan's packet that burst.

Now, mustard does not come out of clothing easily, if at all, and I have often wondered if that nice man thinks of us every time he wears his slightly stained jacket. That's the problem with those little mistakes we make in life… we are sorry, we try to make amends, and we sometimes have gentle reminders – like mustard stains – to keep us from making the same mistake twice.

— Did We Land, Or Wuz We Shot Down? —

We were on our way home from Germany, where we had spent a delightful week with my parents while Johannes attended a medical meeting. The flight over had been delightful – smooth and uneventful. The flight home was another matter entirely. My folks were staying an extra week to tour more of the German countryside, but we had five kids at home, and could afford no such luxury, either in time or money. So here we were on a bumpy ride from Frankfurt to Dulles Airport in Washington, DC.

Now, I am a nervous flyer on the smoothest of flights, and in order to calm myself, I draw. The idea is very similar to Lamaze for the woman in labor – it gives the person something else to think about. Believe me, I didn't stop drawing during the entire 8-hour flight, except perhaps for having a bite to eat. The last hour of the flight was what in German is called, *stark Windig* – strong winds – and our plane lurched all over the sky. The more turbulent it became, the more intricate my drawing became. I still have the drawing, and it reminds me of that flight whenever I see it.

I am a nervous flyer, it is true; but the man two rows behind us put new meaning to the word 'nervous'. Perhaps 'frantic' would be a better term for his condition. As the flight got bumpier, he got more inebriated and louder. "I think that wing is coming off!" he screamed. Even I knew the wing wasn't coming off… His seat mate tried to calm him by explaining that we would be down soon. "I know we're going down!" he shouted hysterically. His final exclamation was the best of all: "I wonder if it would be better if I was running when we crash?" At this point, the entire back of the plane broke into laughter.

That laughter broke our fear, and we vaulted onto the runway in a better frame of mind, thanks to the poor fellow in the last row. It's funny how the Lord answers prayer, isn't it? I had been praying the whole flight, not only for safety, but for allaying of my fears; and the Lord answered those prayers in a pretty unconventional manner!

The Totaled Woman

—— How to Change the World ——

"I think every man ought to be pregnant for a 24-hour period!" I pontificated grandly as I arrived home from running errands. We were expecting a baby, and I had just gone to retrieve the mail from the mailroom at the medical center before starting to cook dinner.

Johannes gave me a quizzical look, which was all I needed to launch into the subject. Now, I must explain that at this stage I truly felt as if pregnancy were a terminal illness. I had gained almost 50 pounds, and was able to just touch my two middle fingers after stretching my arms around my abdomen, which had assumed the shape of a giant oblong watermelon. People no longer looked me in the eye, they looked at my lurching belly. Neither Johannes nor I could sleep because the baby thought nighttime was the time for soccer practice, or at the very least, for calisthenics; the entire bed shuddered all night long.

As I pulled up to the medical center, I took the liberty of parking in the handicapped-parking area right next to the entrance. As I waddled toward the entrance, I passed a man leaving the building. He looked at my car, looked at me, and remarked, "Well, aren't you special! You don't look handicapped to me, lady." I smiled between my teeth and trudged on.

As I entered the elevator, another fellow of low breeding took one look at me and shouted, "You aren't going to have that baby in here, are you?" I didn't bother to smile.

One of Johannes' classmates met me as I exited the elevator, "You look as if you are going to pop!"

My response was, "No, Tony, Johannes is the pop"

Finally, I neared the mailroom…sorry I had ever undertaken the errand. As I rounded the corner, I met my obstetrician, who burst out laughing when he saw me. He apologized profusely, which helped not at all. Actually, it would have been better if he had said nothing. I mean, I could then have thought he was laughing at a joke, or at something in his mail. His apology made it clear that I was what was so hilarious.

"Yes," I repeated to my husband, "every man should spend 24 hours being pregnant. Either during the nausea period, or the not-sleeping period, or the big-as-a-whale period; perhaps during labor, or during delivery…it would change the world."

Johannes was thoughtful. "Perhaps just thinking of the possibility would change the world," he replied.

—— Again? ——

The phone rang as I was trying to find the bottom of the pile of dirty dishes soaking in the kitchen sink.

"Hello, Mrs. Veldhuis? This is Susie in the athletic office at George Mason University; we have talked before on other occasions when Nathan has been injured on the soccer field, remember?"

"Yes, I remember those calls. What is the matter? Is Nathan hurt?"

"Oh he is just fine, an ambulance has transported him on a backboard to the emergency room; but he is just fine."

"If he is fine, then why are you calling?"

"The coach just wanted me to let you know that there is concern that Nathan has broken his neck, but I'm sure he is just fine."

Nathan was goalkeeper on a Division I soccer team. We received such calls more times than a mother wants to acknowledge or remember. Nathan was all right, as it turned out. It was not as serious as the time he dove into the goal post and spent the night in the ICU; or when he was cleated in the mouth and developed a serious infection.

Being the mother of a goalkeeper keeps a mother on her knees, but calls like the one from Susie irritate a mother beyond belief. I mean, really! How dumb can a person be, to call with such a message and then say it is all okay?

Do I try to sugar-coat life's hard lessons, when the pure and simple truth is needed?

The Totaled Woman

—— Escaped! ——

Stefan was four. He was adorable, precocious and indulged by all the older folks at church. In the past few Sundays, Stefan had eluded his father's watch – Dad had several others to keep track of – and found his way from the church pew to the piano bench, cuddling up beside me while I played. Not only was this distracting for me, it was a source of indulgent humor for the congregation. After the third such episode, I laid down the law: no more sitting with Mommy at the piano!

The next Sunday, I extracted a solemn promise from Johannes that he would indeed keep Stefan in his seat, and not allow any more wanderings about the sanctuary. I was relieved, and played with a new confidence, knowing all was well. It was my turn to provide the special music, so after singing the song, I set the microphone on the floor of the platform and sprinted back to the piano during the pastoral prayer. As the prayer ended, we opened our eyes to behold little Stefan, microphone in hand standing at the front of the sanctuary. Our dear pastor walked forward and picked this little blond boy up, holding him while Stefan sang an entire verse of *Seek Ye First*. The congregation was charmed, Stefan was pleased, I glowered at his father who smiled sheepishly as he left the pew to retrieve the escapee. Stefan looked at his dad and said, "But Dad, I didn't go to sit at the piano!"

It never happened again; Johannes was so thankful that his little boy had picked a hymn to sing, and not one of the ditties his older brother and sisters might have taught him!

—— Peanut Butter ——

We were visiting my folks in Idaho, along with my brother and his family. Nathan and Ingrid were little, and were eager for breakfast. Grandmother always seemed to take so long to get the meals ready, although they certainly were delicious when she finally served them.

All was in readiness, except we were waiting for Granddad to stir the peanut butter — they had the fancy kind from the health-food store — not the cheap stuff we had at our house. Granddad disappeared into the garage, which was right out the door from the kitchen. We waited quite awhile; finally my mom decided to go see what was taking so long…she came back laughing, but didn't explain anything.

A few minutes later, my dad — a tall thin man — entered the kitchen in his underwear! Obviously chagrined, he said, "Pardon me," and walked through the dining room and the living room to get to their bedroom, where he shut the door. He reappeared momentarily fully clothed in a new outfit.

Only then did we learn that Dad had used the electric paint stirrer to stir the peanut butter. This would not have been a problem, and was really a great way to do it, except that he lifted up the stirrer while it was still running to see if it was mixed enough…not only did the PB go all over his clothes, it shot a wide swath into the pegboard at the back of the workbench. My mom would not save him from his predicament, but came back from the garage laughing, and left him to figure out what to do next. Our kids were wide-eyed as they saw their distinguished granddad come through the garage door in his skivvies.

Dad and I had some good father-daughter time over the next couple of days, as we dug peanut butter out of the pegboard with screwdrivers.

The Totaled Woman

—— Yes, Olivia, There Is a Santa Claus ——

It was Christmastime. Everyone was full of secrets and excitement. The older kids were old enough to know how it really was, and yet young enough to enjoy keeping the Santa Claus secret for the younger kids.

The discussion around the table as the kids had their snack after school was about Santa. All agreed that he was indeed real, and that he would be coming to visit the Veldhuis house on Christmas Eve. Olivia had been plying us with questions about the jolly old elf as of late…weren't Mommy and Daddy actually Santa? There weren't really reindeer, were there? He didn't really come down the chimney, did he? Our answers had been truthful, although, I admit, oblique, allowing for just one more year of innocence.

One difficulty for Olivia in this regard was that she was two years younger than her classmates, so even though she was in the fourth grade, she was only seven. In the matter of believing in Santa, this was a real disadvantage, as her classmates were more than willing to tell her the truth of it all.

So here we were at snack time. Olivia looked at her little brother, who was five and said, "Stefan, did you know that Mommy and Daddy are really Santa Claus?"

This was too much! I marched Olivia back to our bedroom, closed the door, and said, "Olivia, why would you spoil Santa for your little brother? Nobody spoiled it for you."

Tears came to her big brown eyes... "You mean you really are Santa Claus?" she sobbed.

I had flunked motherhood. No way out of this one. She was testing the waters about Santa, and I had deep-sixed her. We hugged and I told her how sorry I was. As she opened the door, she looked back at me still with tears in her eyes, and said, "I suppose you're the Easter Bunny too."

—— A Family of Drunks ——

One of the advantages of having a father who travels all over the world, is the occasional chance to accompany him. Of course, I could list many disadvantages of having the husband/father traveling so much, but that is not the focus of this glimpse into our lives.

Olivia got an "A" in German, and her dad told her that he would take her with him to Germany on his next trip there. That time has finally come. The plan is for Olivia to stay with a German colleague and his family while Johannes travels to his medical meetings in other areas of the country. Since Olivia is fluent in German, and the Holl family members speak English, this seems like a wonderful arrangement. Did I mention that Olivia is fourteen, and very sheltered…

Her dad saw her safely to the train in Frankfurt, having contacted our friends in Ulm to make sure they would meet her when she arrived. Olivia called home in the middle of the night, in tears. Apparently, on the way home from the train station, they had stopped at the Biergarten for a stein of beer, asking Olivia if she would like one! Now, I hasten to mention that our friends are very nice people…but they do live in Germany where the taste of the water leaves much to be desired, and where there are no age limits for consumption of alcohol. Olivia was devastated; she doesn't even know anyone else who drinks beer, let alone anything stronger. I assured her that all was well; that it was just a cultural difference, and that she was perfectly safe there with those nice people. She felt reassured, and was able to hang up, and drift off to sleep.

Today is Sunday, and the kids and I have been to church. When it was time for congregational prayer requests, little Alisson raised her hand. When the pastor called on her, our five-year-old stood up, and speaking very distinctly, asked us to pray for her sister, Olivia, who was staying in Germany with a family of drunks. As you can imagine, this created quite a stir throughout the congregation. The elder whose job it was to pray for the various requests, shot me a quizzical look. I just smiled weakly, closing my eyes for prayer.

When church ended, I gathered up the kids as quickly as possible, and escaped without stopping to explain anything. No matter what I said at that point, it would look like an excuse, and we all know that there is no excuse good enough for leaving one's daughter with a family of drunks.

The Totaled Woman

— High Flyer —

It was a lovely Sunday morning. As we drove toward the church, we discussed the morning's activities – Johannes' Sunday School class on Ephesians (we'd been in Ephesians for almost a year now, and our Bibles just opened automatically to the correct page), the kids' classes, the choir number that needed a final run-through. I told Johannes that I'd be a few minutes late for Sunday School, since I hadn't had time to play through the prelude before we left…a normal Sunday morning at the Veldhuis home. Sunday School was excellent, and the choir run-through went well: harbingers of a wonderful church morning.

Today we had a pastoral candidate, who was preaching and having lunch with the congregation at a potluck after the service. As I started the prelude, everyone settled down for an inspiring time in God's word…it did seem odd, however, that their attention was focused near the piano. In my experience, the prelude is pretty much considered background music for saying hello to the person next to you, or settling the kids with their children's bulletin and crayons, or wondering what you did with your Bible after Sunday School. But this morning, all eyes were on the piano, which made me a little apprehensive, what was I playing that caused such interest?

The visiting pastor opened with prayer, and the service began. Even during an engaging and lively children's message, the attention seemed focused in the direction of the piano. I thought perhaps there was something on the piano that was attracting everyone's gaze, but after a cursory look around, I saw nothing. Tom, the pastoral candidate, had also noticed the lack of attention to the pulpit, and – as a visiting speaker – was quite disconcerted.

Finally, after the choir sang, I shot a quizzical glance at Johannes, who merely lifted his chin, as if he were looking up...I looked up. Directly above the piano was a light fixture, sort of a translucent shallow bowl fastened several inches from the ceiling. In that light fixture was a body...with pointy wings...trying to get out. It silently, repeatedly pawed its way to the edge of the fixture, and then slid back down. With the light illuminated, the black body was silhouetted dramatically, and every eye in the congregation was watching, wondering if the bat would indeed reach the rim and tumble down to safety. Of course, 'safety' would be on the head of the pianist.

I have never appreciated a sermon quite as much as I did that day, since I was sitting with my family in the pew, and not under the light fixture, which held the climbing creature. Unfortunately, I have no idea what the sermon topic was, or what Tom the visiting preacher said; which was probably true of the whole congregation. Somehow, I forced myself back up to the instrument for the final song, after which I bolted from the piano bench with a shudder.

Apparently, there is no provision in the listing of church responsibilities for whose job it is to remove a live bat from a light fixture. So when we arrived for the evening service, the bat was still there. However, this time he wasn't moving. The body silhouetted in the light fixture was splayed out, and dead. Piano playing was not enjoyable that evening, but the fear was gone.

Remarkably, Tom took the position as our pastor. Amazing how a little thing like a bat can distract us from what should be the important things in life.

—— 'On Call' ——

During the three years of Johannes' medical residency, we house-sat for his dad. His house sat in the woods on five acres, and there were only five houses on the little gravel lane out in the country. We lived 20 miles from the hospital, and Johannes was 'on call' every third night, which meant that he had to stay at the hospital from 7:00 a.m. one day to noon the following day. For that reason, we got a dog, a big dog, with a big bark. In the three years we lived there, I never really slept well when Johannes was gone, but having our husky made me feel a bit more secure at night when the kids and I were home alone.

Minnesota is a cold place. Snow remains on the ground most of the winter, to say nothing of fall and spring. When the temperatures drop below zero, walking on the snow produces a loud squealing sound that can be heard for quite a distance. On this particular day, temperatures hovered between -15 and -20...lots of squealing...in case anyone was foolish enough to be outside.

Johannes was 'on call' and we didn't expect him home until tomorrow at midday, but he surprised us by driving in about 5:30 – just in time for dinner! It was dark by then, but I heard the squealing of the tires on the snow, and ran to open the garage door.

Apparently, whoever made up the 'call' list had made a mistake, and scheduled two residents for the same night ...Johannes did not have call! What a treat! Dinner was a bit lean, since I hadn't expected him, but he didn't complain as I served a 'breakfast dinner' of scrambled eggs and pancakes. He was exhausted, and was just glad to have made it home safely, with all the snow, and more in the forecast.

Ahh, the kids were settled for the night. We scooted into our pajamas, read the Bible together, and turned out the light. We were just drifting off to sleep when there was a loud knock at the front door. Johannes pretended not to hear, while I sat bolt upright and listened…squealing snow! Who could be at the door at 10 o'clock at night, out here in the country, and why was the snow squealing?

The squealing stopped…the garage door opened! Johannes was still feigning sleep, but I wasn't buying it now. "Get up! There is someone trying to get into the house!"

"Oh, don't be silly. It is probably just my brother, Mike."

Now, Mike lives in Florida. It is true that he scared our socks off us when we lived in a mobile home in Hershey and he was en-route back home to Orlando. He needed a place to spend the night, so he drove through Pennsylvania to our house, went around to the back, and pounded on the wall of our bedroom at midnight.

But this was three years later, and this was Minnesota, and this was winter, and this was ridiculous! "Johannes, that is not Mike! Listen! Someone is walking around to the back of the house! Get up!"

Now, either he was not convinced, or he didn't want to be convinced… he got up slowly, and looked for his bathrobe. "You don't need a bathrobe! Hurry! I hear someone on the back porch!"

As we started down the stairs in the dark – I was pushing Johannes ahead of me – we heard our watchdog drinking from the toilet just off the entryway. The sliding glass door slid open. How, you ask, did we know the door was open if it was dark? Remember, it was 20 below zero, and we could feel the cold as soon as the door opened. Suddenly, Johannes shouted, "Who's there?"

A scramble of feet, wild squealing of snow as the intruder ran for his car, which he had parked in the circular driveway. Johannes went to shut the door while I vaulted upstairs to look out the bedroom window, hoping to catch sight of the burglar, or at least determine what kind of car he was driving.

The Totaled Woman

He got stuck twice as he gunned the engine, but finally made it out of the driveway and barreled down the lane out of sight.

When I got back downstairs, Johannes was calling the police. So much for a good night's sleep. The police told us that they had been trying to catch this guy for weeks. His specialty was robbing empty houses, removing all the furniture and any valuables he could find. It seems that living in a lovely house on a five-acre lot made us a target. He knocked at the door, but was quite certain the occupants were in some warmer climate for the winter. He was even more certain when he checked the garage and found only a little VW bug, which he must have assumed was our second car. As for his ease of getting into the house, the police suggested that we put a broom handle in the door track, and buy some dead bolts for the other doors. With that, they wished us a pleasant sleep, and departed...

Of course, we couldn't possibly sleep. Our watchdog was a dud...he never barked, or even came up to the living room to see what was going on. All we could think about was that Johannes was supposed to have been on call that night, 20 miles away. What if I'd been home alone?

I was home alone many nights after that night. But now we had dead bolts and broom handles. Somehow, though, that never really totally reassured me. I found comfort in my prayer life, since it was certain there was no use trusting in the dog to keep me safe.

Perhaps it would be better to just go straight to the Lord, and not trust in the security this world, or a watchdog, offers.

—— Intruder! ——

A week or so after our encounter with the burglar, I had to call the furnace repairman. It is Minnesota in the winter, so you know that fixing the furnace is a top priority. Since I needed the car, I had to take Johannes to the medical center. This meant that I was not going to be there when the repairman came, so I left the door unlocked for him with the understanding that he would lock the door when he left.

When the kids and I returned home some time later, the door into the equipment room was unlocked. The house was quite cold, and there were tools scattered around near the furnace. I assumed that the repairman had gone to retrieve a part, and would be back soon.

My two toddlers helped me bring in the groceries, dropping items as they went. The phone rang. "Hello, Mrs. Veldhuis? This is Fred from Fred's Furnace Company. I just wanted you to know that I will not be back to finish fixing your furnace. Good bye."

"What in the world was that all about?" I mused. Nathan looked at me and asked why it was so cold in the house. I started a fire in the fireplace, and gathered playthings nearby so the kids could stay warm. I was not so fortunate, since the laundry room and kitchen were nowhere near the fireplace.

Just then, the doorbell rang. It was our friendly neighbor, Shirley, from across the street. She just wanted to let me know that there had been a strange truck in our driveway while I was gone, so she had called the police. She was watching out for us. I told her that it actually had just been a repairman, but thanked her for keeping such good watch for us.

When I called the furnace man back to ask him what had happened, I didn't blame him for never wanting to come back. It seems that while he was working on the furnace, with his back to the door leading into the garage, a policeman entered quietly and accosted him with his pistol drawn.

Johannes struggled with that furnace the rest of the time we lived there. True to his word, Fred never did return – even for the tools he'd left behind.

The Bogey Man

Whenever we go on a trip that requires staying in a hotel, we encounter the bogey man. Unlike a troll, who resides under bridges, the bogey man makes his abode in hotels, especially near the drink and snack machines.

When traveling by car with a crew of kids, one must be imaginative to keep the masses happy and entertained... thus, the bogey man at the end of a long day of driving. After dinner, baths and pajamas, Daddy and kids prepare to meet this phantom, wherever he might be. They sneak down the hall, quarters and ice bucket in hand, looking for the drink machine. Suddenly, their dad smacks the door of the elevator and takes off at a run. The kids all jump, and shout, "the bogey man!" and take off after their dad. Next, Dad lurches toward the exit, with a shout, and they run down another hall. This little game goes on for at least ten minutes while they search for the coveted drink machine – which, of course, they have located long ago.

On our last trip, I decided to enter the fun. They returned from their adventure with their drinks, Nathan as the eldest, carrying the ice bucket so they could divide the drinks into glasses and add a little ice. Hmm, where was Mom?

Now there are not many places to hide in a little hotel room, so the search for Mom began. They looked in the closet...nope. How about under the bed...wrong again. Behind the curtain...definitely not there. Let's check the bathroom...as Nathan pulled back the shower curtain, I leaned forward from where I was standing in the bathtub and said quietly in a low voice, "Bogey, bogey, bogey!" Nathan, still holding the ice bucket filled with ice, threw the bucket in the air, and collapsed on the floor.

They had finally found the bogey man.

A Blood of Pool

We were at the hotel. Kids were settling down for the night. We had adjoining rooms, with the older kids in one, the baby and parents in the other. Of course, the door between was open. Johannes was reading the Bible with the older ones while I tended to Alisson, who was just a baby. Johannes had a way of bringing the Bible stories to life, so that the kids felt they had entered into the story themselves; they always looked forward to this time of day.

As they came into our room to say good night after Bible reading and prayer time, each child had a wide-eyed look, which did not seem conducive to slumber. "What story did you guys talk about tonight?" I inquired.

"The battle of Armageddon," Nathan replied somberly.

"Yeah," Stefan blurted out, "and about the Beast."

"The Beast?" I asked incredulously…I mean this was the kids' beforebed Bible story, for Heaven's sake.

"Well, that's what he said, Mom!" added Olivia. "He was really excited about it!"

I looked at Johannes, who confirmed with a nod that what the kids said was the way it was.

"Okay, kids. Say good night to your mother. It's time for bed." Johannes herded the group toward their room. "Stefan, be sure to lock the door."

"Aw, Dad, why do we need to lock the door? Nobody is going to bother us in a nice place like this."

"Well, Stefan, would you like to wake up in a blood of pool in the morning? If not, I suggest you lock the door." We all burst out laughing; Dad had obviously mixed up the words, and said it backwards, but added to the evening's Bible story, it served to augment the apprehension of the evening.

The kids were up and in our room variously throughout the night. Perhaps tonight Johannes will pick a psalm, or discuss how Jesus loves the little children. We've had enough 'blood of pool' for awhile.

—— Mac the Knife ——

The day before Olivia was born, I promised Ingrid that I would trim her hair the very next day. She was three, and finally had some hair to trim. Of course, babies come whenever they are ready, and not when we expect them; at least that's the way it's been at this house, so my promise was indeed ill-timed.

New Year's Day brought the beautiful baby girl who was supposed to have been born the middle of December. January 2nd I returned home, ready to tackle life with a sweet, but exhausted husband who spent much of his life at the hospital, and three little children who spent all of their time vying for my attention.

The morning after I got home, I awoke (of course, with a newborn, the word 'awoke' would apply to the entire night), staggering downstairs to find the children. Nathan and Ingrid were nowhere to be found! The front door was still locked, so they hadn't left the house. Oh, what about the sliding glass door? Better check that.

We lived in a townhouse, and our sliding door faced our little porch and then the back of another townhouse. In other words, there was no privacy in that direction unless we had the curtain drawn. The curtain was drawn, but I could hear voices, even though I saw no one. Pulling back the curtain, I discovered Nathan and Ingrid, stark naked, holding my large, very sharp sewing scissors and a long, sharp Ginsu carving knife.

Nathan, at age four-and-a-half, was very proud of himself as he announced, "Mommy, I cut Ingrid's hair for you!" Now, Nathan was born with a luxuriant head of thick wavy hair, but Ingrid had been working on the modest amount she had for three full years. He sensed that Mommy was not happy: "Mommy, remember you told Ingrid you were going to cut her hair. But you've been gone, so I did it for you. We even took off our pajamas so we wouldn't get hair on them." I held out my hand, and he gave me the knife. Ingrid handed me the scissors.

My endocrinologist husband tells me that after childbirth, a woman's hormones go through terrific changes. Well, my hormones just collapsed when I saw Ingrid's lovely hair all over the floor, to say nothing of the disaster effected by giant sewing scissors in the hands of a four-year-old. How Nathan avoided severing his sister's ear, I will never know. The part I had meant to trim before Olivia's birth, her bangs, were no more…cut to the quick. What might our darling little girl have looked like if I hadn't interrupted this tonsorial disaster? I shudder to imagine.

The hormones reached rock bottom, and I burst into tears – a disconcerting thing for the little helpers. They sprinted up the stairs to their rooms and shut their doors, obviously unable to understand Mommy's strange behavior when they had been so helpful.

I collapsed into a chair in the living room, where reality came upon me gradually. What were all these electrostatic beads on the floor? Millions of them, it seemed. Where was the giant bean bag we kept at the bottom of the kids' slide? And, come to think of it, what was Nathan doing with that huge carving knife? I found the bean bag behind the couch, unzipped and emptied of its contents. The answer to the knife question lay in the several pieces of the once-whole curtain cord lying near where I had found the kids. How or why he climbed up onto the kitchen counter to get it, I have no clue.

When Johannes woke up, he couldn't believe the disaster perpetrated by two little children. He cleaned as much of the bean-bag contents as he could with the snow shovel, although we discovered hidden pockets of them up to the time we moved a year later.

Nathan and Ingrid had no idea of the danger of their endeavors. They were just experimenting with what they perceived as a newfound freedom and ability. With parents upstairs asleep, they decided to take matters into their own hands…the lesson here is compelling, even to the adults cleaning up the mess.

　　　　　　　　　　　　　　The Totaled Woman

—— Mrs. H. ——

Mrs. H. was a dear friend. When we first met her she was 80 years old, frail and had been a widow for many years. Most of the church folks were a little afraid of her, we found out over the years; but her heart was full of the Savior's love, even if her manner was brusque.

One of my first memories of her was at church one Sunday when Stefan was a baby. She marched up to me after the service and asked, "Just how long do you intend to breast feed that baby?"

Another time, when Johannes was out of town attending one of his many medical meetings, she took me aside after Sunday School and said, "Well, you'd better be sure to keep looking good, because if you aren't careful, he'll trade you in for a younger model now that you've had all those kids."

Yes, Mrs. H. was a character, but we loved her dearly. We told her as we dropped her off at her apartment after church one Sunday, that we were planning to take her out to lunch the following Saturday for her 85th birthday, and had picked a nice place that served delicious chocolate cake. "I don't like to go out to eat." she responded, "I'm going to just stay home in my housecoat and listen to some nice music."

"Well, Mrs. H.," said Johannes, not the least bit perturbed, "I suggest you have on something other than your housecoat, because we will be by at noon to take you to lunch."

"There are too many steps to climb," she replied doggedly, "and I don't like cake."

"I've been by the restaurant and counted them, Mrs. H, and there are only three."

Saturday came, and we were at Mrs. H's door right on time. She answered the door with a smile, dressed to the nines and ready to go. She had a wonderful time, and ate a huge piece of chocolate cake.

Although she didn't mention that first birthday lunch again, each succeeding year when her birthday rolled around, she met us with a smile and dressed in her best clothes, when we called to take her to lunch.

—— At My Worst ——

Mrs. H's sons were coming from across the country to visit her. She was now in her 90s and unable do much cooking. She had moved into an assisted-living apartment and took her meals in their dining facility. But her boys were coming, and she wanted to have a home-cooked dinner for them when they arrived.

I visited her every Sunday afternoon. She would sit in her easy chair while I sat on her floor chatting while preparing the latest bulletin board for my classroom, or collating test papers. It helped us pass the time, and provided a relaxed atmosphere. Sometimes, she would ask me to play her piano, since she could play it no longer. Other times I'd whip up something she fancied in her little kitchen. Today we were talking about her two boys.

"Why don't I just fix dinner for the three of you?" I asked, "I'll just bring it over in the afternoon, so you will have everything you need when they arrive from the airport." And that is what I did.

On the day of her sons' arrival, I scurried around, loading the dinner, dessert and some homemade coffee cake for their breakfast the following morning into a box in the back of the car. I gave my hair a quick brush — fastening it back from my face with a little clip — pulled on one of the boys' oversized T-shirts, and drove off to Mrs. H's.

After juggling my load carefully, I could reach her knocker. I heard her walker squeak as she made her way to the door. "Hello, Mrs. H., here I am with the dinner!"

She stood in the doorway and looked at me. I mean really looked at me. She stared at my scruffy tennis shoes and silently examined my jeans, oversized T-shirt, my hair…everything. Then she paused, looking me straight in the eye and said, "Now I've seen you at your worst."

By this time, we had known Mrs. H. for many years, and I just laughed as I stood there with dinner for three, dessert and breakfast. She finally opened the door enough for me to come in and set down my load. The meal met with her approval, even if my attire didn't, and she smiled and thanked me as I prepared to scoot home.

"You'd better hurry up and leave before the boys see you looking like that," she said as she shut the door.

—— That's 'D' as in Death ——

As the years passed, Mrs. H. thought more and more about death. Not in a morbid way, but in a practical way that suited her very practical personality. As she approached her 95th birthday, we noticed a new urgency in her preparations for her passage to be with her Savior.

She had a manila folder with her wishes for her funeral all neatly typed out. As she got more frail, she asked me to type the things she wished to add or change. She fretted greatly over one of her sons, whom she was afraid, did not know the Lord. Her funeral plans were focused around giving the clear Gospel message to her boy.

"So now, here is the song I want you to sing, Marcia." She handed me a page of music.

I looked at her incredulously. "Mrs. H., what do you think I am? You are my dear friend, I could never sing at your funeral – I'd never make it through the song. I will play the piano, but I will not be able to sing."

She gave me a strange look, as if such emotion had never occurred to her, but she didn't argue. She just said, "Well, you'd better get out the folder then, and we'll change that part of the service."

I went over to her little filing cabinet and looked for the file without success. "Mrs. H., I don't seem to find that folder, did you leave it out on your desk maybe?"

"No, it is in the filing cabinet, just keep looking." I looked in the 'F' file, assuming she'd entitled the folder 'funeral'...no luck. So, next I checked 'M' for 'memorial service'...nope. Maybe it was under 'P' for 'passing'. Still no luck.

"Mrs. H., I can't seem to find it anywhere."

"Well, what are you looking under?" I told her, and she looked quite exasperated. "Try looking under 'D'."

"'D'?" I asked skeptically.

"Well, 'D' is for 'Death' of course!"

She died within the year, and her funeral gave all the glory to the God she served.

The Totaled Woman

── We Finally Got Some Sense ──

Johannes and I met in college, and we'd been engaged for almost a year. His family lived in Florida, I lived in Idaho; this was the second summer we had spent apart. We were through with college, and Johannes was soon leaving for medical school in Pennsylvania.

We had worked it all out…Johannes was going to fly out to Idaho to see me, and become more acquainted with my parents. We were then going to drive across the country in my car. Johannes would live in the medical-student housing; I had secured a little apartment in a nearby town, and would look for a job. I had made reservations at hotels all the way across the country – two rooms. It was expensive, but it was proper. We were planning a June wedding the following summer.

September 3rd, Johannes called, as he did almost every night. We discussed his arrival on the 11th and our departure on the 13th. How the conversation turned to marriage, I cannot tell you. He mentioned that maybe we should get married in March, during Spring Break. I said, "Wonderful."

"Well," he continued, "maybe we should get married at Christmas, that's a nice time for a wedding."

"Even better!" I said.

"Your birthday is at Thanksgiving. What if we got married then?"

"I'd love that!" I was getting pretty excited about now.

"Well, you know, we probably should just get married before I start medical school."

"Yessss!"

We had a brief moment of sanity as we realized that we'd better talk with our folks. So we hung up, promising to talk again in a half hour.

My folks were getting ready for bed. I knocked and went into their bedroom. "What would you think if there was a little change of plans?" I asked hesitantly.

"When are you getting married?" my mom asked.

"Next week?" I stammered.

"I am so glad you finally got some sense!" said my dad.

Mom bounded out of bed, grabbed her big blue *Emily Post Etiquette Guide* and we started to hand-write wedding invitations. Johannes and I were married a week later.

Our parents were wise. They never told us how dumb it would be to take off across the country to live without being married. They let us come to that conclusion ourselves. Only after we'd made our own decision did they let us know what they thought.

May we show as much wisdom with our children as our parents have shown with us.

—— The College Girl ——

It was Alisson's first year of college. The phone rang. "Hey Mom! You'll never guess what I found on my walk this afternoon."

Now Alisson is a poetic soul, so I assumed she would describe a beautiful tree, or perhaps tell me about a lovely pond she had discovered. "I can't guess, Alisson. What did you find?"

"A squirrel!"

A squirrel? Why is that worth a phone call home? We see those every day, for Heaven's sake.

"Oh…a squirrel…that's nice."

"No Mom, you don't understand. This is a sick squirrel, and he's just a baby. He looked so sad, and he isn't at all well, I can tell."

"Aw, poor little thing. I hope the mother squirrel takes good care of him until he is better."

"No need for that, Mom. I brought him home with me."

Brought him home?

"Alisson! You have no idea how to take care of a sick animal in your dorm room!"

"Sure I do, Mom. I have him all wrapped up in a blanket, and I set him next to the heater in my room. He surely does look sick though"

In a blanket? In your room?

"Alisson, that isn't safe! You don't have any idea what has made him sick!"

"Not to worry, Mom. I've been reading up on squirrels, and I'm doing all the right things. This website even tells some different sicknesses squirrels can get. Hmm, do you know anything about rabies?"

The Totaled Woman   89

—— Of Flags and Hugs ——

When Johannes and I married, he was a Canadian citizen. During our first year of marriage, he determined to seek U.S. citizenship. He filled out all the proper forms, contacted the appropriate acquaintances to write letters attesting to his being an upright person, and made an appointment with the immigration office to schedule his in-person interview. One problem was, having just moved to Pennsylvania, we really didn't know anybody who could stand in as a character witness for him during the interview. I certainly knew that he was a character, but wives weren't allowed to be witnesses.

We had just moved into a mobile home set in what was grandly called a mobile-home park. Two trailers away lived another medical-student couple whom we had met once or twice. Bill and MiMi have been our dear friends for years now, but then we barely knew their names. Bill, however, agreed to spend a morning in Harrisburg at the immigration office, swearing to Johannes' fine upstanding character. This part of the process went off without a hitch. They asked Johannes very important questions every citizen ought to know: how many states were there in the US; who was the governor of Pennsylvania; where is the US capital…deep stuff.

The next step was his meeting with the Prothonotary of the Court. We went together for this truly Dickensian experience. At the courthouse, we entered a strange chamber lighted only by an ancient desk lamp, which illuminated a portion of an oak desk behind which sat a wizened man. It was difficult to distinguish his features in the dim yellowish light, but as we

The Totaled Woman

approached and took the chairs he offered, our eyes became accustomed to the gloom, and we were able to see a little man engulfed by enormous black-rimmed glasses sitting behind a mammoth desk, surrounded by papers. He asked a few questions about Johannes' background and plans for the future, why we were living in Pennsylvania, and the interview was over. The gentleman never really raised his eyes to make eye contact. He looked at his papers, spoke in almost a whisper, and dismissed us by stamping an official paper and handing it to Johannes.

The day of the swearing-in finally came. The woman sitting next to us in the courtroom was from Cuba, and was fairly overcome with emotion. The clerk of the court announced the arrival of the prothonotary, who looked a bit less wizened in the light of the courtroom; we all stood as the judge entered.

What should have been an hour's ceremony took over three hours. Everyone was retiring that day – the clerk, the prothonotary and the judge – and each one felt it necessary to make a speech. Finally, the applicants were called one-by-one to come before the judge and be declared citizens of the United States. Since Veldhuis is at the end of the alphabet, we had time to watch all the others go before Johannes' turn. I leaned over and whispered, "All that's missing is the ladies from the DAR with little American flags." At exactly that moment, a little door flew open at the side of the judge's platform, and out marched a group of elderly ladies bearing little flags!

After all had been sworn in, the ladies started down the row to present each new citizen with a flag. There was much hugging and crying as they made their way to the end of the line. Now, Johannes is a dignified sort, and as an elderly lady in a walker approached him with a flag, obviously intending to give him a hug, he shot out his hand to shake hers, almost knocking her down. "How do you do?" he said formally, bowing a bit at the waist.

Johannes is quite the hugger these days. However, I doubt if even now he would embrace a little old lady he didn't know, even if she were proffering an American flag.

—— Out of Gas ——

We'd been married five days. All our possessions were packed in a little U-Haul trailer attached to the back of the car. The five-day trip across the country was our first adventure together, and we were excited to get underway. Johannes had to be in Hershey for the start of medical school the following week, so there was little leeway in our travel time; but we were newlyweds and in love, and knew no worries.

Our car was a red Impala two-door coupe with a big engine, which required a good deal of fuel. We filled up with gas before starting through the mountains of Utah knowing that it was a long stretch between towns and filling stations, but pulling a trailer used more gas than just driving the car itself. As we approached Snowville, the car spluttered, lurched and died. Johannes managed to steer it to the side of the road. Now Snowville was then basically a service station and a bar, and is located between two sets of mountains. The road was straight and level as we approached; we could see the service station ahead, but ran out of gas about 200 yards before we reached it.

There was absolutely no traffic on the road, so Johannes jumped out, and walked to the service station while I stayed with the car. When he returned with a little red gas can, he explained what had taken him so long…the guy at the gas station insisted that Johannes give him a $10 non-refundable deposit for the gas can! Now, we were newlyweds, and we were poor, and $10 was a lot of money. Besides, where did the fellow think we could go on two gallons of gas? After all, we had a hundred more miles to go through the mountains with no gas stations until we reached Ogden. Johannes poured the gas into the tank, started the car and pulled up to the gas station.

With a full tank, we headed off through the mountains; but something was definitely the matter with the car now. It would not go out of first gear. We were certainly not going back to the station in Snowville. We figured that guy would charge us just to look under the hood, so we drove through the mountains all the way to Ogden in first gear.

It was Sunday night when we limped our way into Ogden and found an open service station. The proprietor was a nice man who was willing to help us. He called around right then and located a used transmission, assuring us that he would have the transmission replaced by Monday at noon. True to his word, the car was ready on time, and we were good to go.

Now it was time to pay for the transmission. We had just enough money to make it across the country, with no contingency money at all. Actually, we had no way to pay him! No checking account, no extra funds, nothing. As I searched through my wallet for what I knew wasn't there, the fellow stopped me, "There! What is that?"

"Oh, I don't know," I replied, "it's some card they sent me last year when I was in college."

It was a MasterCard! He ran it through, and we were on our way. We agreed that we were not going to tell our folks about this, since we were now married and on our own. We didn't want them to worry.

Twenty years later, we were finally telling my folks, thinking they'd enjoy hearing something we'd kept hidden so long. "Oh, we knew about it the day it happened." said Mom, "The bank called us to ask if it was a legitimate charge."

We try to keep matters in our own hands and take care of things ourselves, when the Lord – and our mothers – know all along.

—— Two Perfect People ——

Naivete, that's what it was. There were two perfect men in my life now, and they were about to meet. I had told my dad every wonderful aspect of the young man I loved; I had told Johannes every perfect thing about my dad.

Dad had a business meeting within driving distance of the college, and had rented a car so he could meet this young man I loved so dearly. So, as Johannes and I walked from the college to Dad's hotel, my hopes were high that our evening would be just wonderful...wrong.

Dad was waiting for us in the lobby. As the men shook hands, Johannes asked, "So, how did your meeting go?"

"Well, it wasn't really a meeting," Dad responded precisely.

"I see. What exactly do you call a gathering of people for a specific purpose?" Johannes asked crisply.

The conversation went along in this vein for several miserable minutes until we finally reached Dad's rental car, and started on our way to the restaurant for dinner. Dad wisely changed the topic, and began an explanation of floe meters...bad idea...Johannes certainly knew what a floe meter was, and told Dad so.

Dinner was no better as the two perfect men felt each other out, knowing full well that the other fellow was not perfect, or even close to it. The Chinese dishes arrived at our table. I took one bite and my lips and tongue began to swell like a balloon. Nerves do amazing things, and my nerves were in high gear that night.

Johannes had picked a good movie for us to see. He explained that it was about scientists who were able to shrink themselves so that they could enter a man's body, going through the blood stream, and repairing damage that would otherwise kill the person. The movie we actually saw was about a dog and a cat journeying back home after being left miles away. One was called *The Incredible Journey*, the other *The Incredible Voyage*. Johannes was embarrassed, Dad was tolerant.

The entire evening was an incredible journey. Men are competitive I learned that night; they test the mettle of the opponent to see what stuff he is made of. Johannes and my dad were dear friends until my dad died; they had tested each other's mettle and found it worthy.

—— Emergency! ——

It was Tuesday, and I was at the community-wide Bible study at a large church in town. Olivia and Stefan were in the nursery provided for children of the ladies attending the study, and I was relishing the company of people over the age of seven.

"Marcia Veldhuis, you have an emergency call in the church office." It was the church secretary standing at the door of the room where sat over 100 women. An audible gasp escaped the group as I hurried from the room, wondering if Nathan or Ingrid had been hurt at school, or one of them were sick.

It was Johannes. Everyone was fine, but our friend Fran had called the house unexpectedly on her way back to Pennsylvania. Johannes is almost never home in the middle of the day, but he was working feverishly on a grant. Fran had expected me to answer the phone, but Johannes invited her to come by the house for lunch and a chat. Even though Fran is a happily married Christian woman, my proper husband knew that it was not right to entertain a woman in his home without his wife. He then made his frantic call to the church. The ever-efficient and somewhat supercilious secretary told him that she couldn't interrupt the Bible study unless there was an emergency. To him it was indeed an emergency so he said, "This is Dr. Veldhuis, and we have a family emergency."

As I hung up the phone, the secretary was staring at me quizzically. I just smiled and left the office. It was not that easy for me to extricate myself from the ladies of the Bible study, however. I entered the room to retrieve my purse and Bible just as they were in prayer for "Marcia, and whatever emergency has befallen her family." I sprinted for the door, but didn't make it before the "Amen." My explanation was brief and vague: my family members were all right, but there was an unusual emergency at home, which required my immediate attention.

We have since had real emergencies…broken legs, illness, lost children. We pretty much handled those alone with the Lord. This was the only time we had a built-in prayer meeting that numbered a hundred.

Humor…where would we be without it?

──── It's Definitely Broken ────

What a wonderful day to be outside! Sunny, temperatures in the 80s, a perfect day to mow the lawn while the kids play in the hose. We have a perfect hill where the kids can set down a long piece of plastic sheeting and put the hose so the water runs down the plastic. The children run along the grass up to the plastic, take a flying leap and slide as if they were on ice. It is a slippery, fun way to cool off on a hot summer's day. I mow the lawn while they play in the water.

After they had made a few runs, Nathan came around the side of the house carrying Stefan in his arms. A mother has a certain sense when it comes to her children. I turned off the lawn mower at once, Stefan was obviously hurt.

"What happened, Nathan?"

"Nothing, Mom. Stefan was just standing there, and he slipped on the wet plastic and sat down on his leg."

It sounded minor, but it looked major. Stefan's face told me that. I certainly wished his father were home, but Johannes was out of the country. In such circumstances, one deals with the crisis and falls apart later.

Physician's wives are among the most helpless in times of medical need. When Ingrid had a reaction to her MMR immunization and had a fever of 105, Johannes got home from the hospital and put her in a cool bath. When Stefan broke his teeth, Johannes took him to the dentist. When Nathan dropped his desk on his foot and broke his toe, Johannes knew just what to do. But here I was with no idea what to do, and I could not reach him by phone to ask.

It was dusk by the time I got the kids in the car and drove around the block to the house of a physician neighbor, who told me, "Take that boy to the hospital." As I said, doctors' wives tend to be a bit helpless, and I needed someone to tell me what I really already knew. I left the kids at our pastor's home, and drove Stefan to the hospital emergency room, where they x-rayed his leg and confirmed my fears. He had a spiral break of both bones in his right lower leg. Later that night we left the hospital with Stefan sporting a cast all the way to his hip. Have I mentioned that Stefan was not yet three? He broke his leg a week before his third birthday, and spent most of the summer in a cast.

We carried him wherever he wanted or needed to go, since he was too little to handle crutches. Actually, that time in the cast was no problem compared to the months after the cast was removed. He was just a little guy, and he really hadn't been doing anything except standing there when he broke his leg. So, he was afraid to walk after they took the cast off. He would scoot around the house on his bottom, much like a crab. As the weeks went by, Johannes worried that Stefan's leg would atrophy without proper exercise and movement, so on a Saturday we took the kids to the mall. We splurged on lunch in a restaurant, and made sure to sit at the very back. When we finished our meal, I took the other kids and went out into the mall, leaving Stefan and his dad to make their way out to join us. Johannes would not carry him, and Stefan would not walk...it took one-half hour for them to slowly make their way from the back of the restaurant into the mall. Stefan would hold his daddy's hand and take a step then sit down crying, take another step and then sit down.

Johannes was wise, he never shamed his little boy; he just held his hand until he was ready to take another step. Stefan slowly began to trust his daddy to help him walk, and within a week, he was running around the house as if nothing had happened.

What a picture of our walk with the Savior. When we are afraid, He waits patiently for us to take the next step in faith and trust.

—— A Concatenation of Platitudes ——

Fridays were usually our 'date nights', but it hadn't worked out this week, so it was Saturday, and we were out on the town, which at this stage – what we call early poverty – meant a slice of pizza at Maria's Pizza Parlor.

I was able to get Margie, our favorite babysitter, so we were dawdling over our pizza, and just enjoying each other's company after a busy week. As we drove home, we noticed a car parked in front of our house. Assuming it was someone visiting our next-door-neighbor, we drove up into the garage.

As we were getting out of the car, Johannes felt his contact lens flip out. I came around to help him look for it, turning on the garage light as I passed the switch. We were both bent over feeling for the contact – Johannes searching the car, I was checking out the garage floor. For some reason I looked up toward the open garage door…there stood a man I had never seen before. He was not moving or speaking – just standing there looking at us.

Without moving, I said quietly to Johannes, "There is a strange man standing in the garage." At that moment, Johannes located his contact, and stood up triumphantly to greet this perfect stranger.

"Hello," he said, shaking Johannes' hand, "You don't know me, but I wrote you a letter last year. My name is Alfred Aspic. I was in town on a business trip and thought I'd just drop by."

Being a natural born chicken, I dove into the house to check with Margie and see how the kids had done while we were gone. Margie was totally unnerved. No, the kids were all asleep, no problem there; but there was some strange man skulking around the outside of the house, so she had called her parents, who had called the police.

As Johannes came in from the garage, Alfred came in behind him. Johannes explained that he was sorry, but he needed to get the babysitter home, and then we would be going to bed. Alfred said, "No problem, I'll just

100   The Totaled Woman

relax in your living room until you get back." I took my cue, and offered to take the babysitter home.

I had to reassure Margie's parents that the man in front of the house had come to visit us. I really couldn't say much more, since we had no idea who he was. My sweet husband was putting on a pot of coffee when I returned. Alfred wondered if we were going to be having dessert, by any chance, because he would certainly enjoy having some too. Johannes and I exchanged helpless glances, and I started preparing some fresh strawberries to put on our little dishes of ice cream. I asked Alfred which he would prefer, berries or chocolate syrup. He said he would like both, thanks. By now, it was after 10:00, and I was tired. I handed him the ice cream, the strawberries and the chocolate sauce and said, "You'll have to fix that yourself."

He polished off the coffee and dessert, and we stood as Johannes shook his hand and thanked him for stopping by. Alfred smiled and said, "Oh, if you don't mind, I think I'll spend the night. It's too late for me to start driving home now."

Sunday morning came, and Mr. Aspic was still with us. All morning, he followed me around the kitchen saying, "Have you complimented your mirror lately." He was a strange bird, to say the least. He showed no sign of preparing to leave, so we invited him to church...a big mistake. At the time designated for introducing visitors, Johannes rose to introduce Mr. Aspic, but Alfred jumped to his feet and interrupted him, introducing himself and going on for three or four minutes telling all sorts of things about his work and where he lived.

We thought we were thoroughly embarrassed at that point, but that was nothing compared to what happened after the service. As he shook the pastor's hand, he said, "I enjoyed your metaphor about the watch, but the rest of what you said was just a concatenation of platitudes."

Alfred drove off, and we have never seen him again...which is just fine with us.

—— Random Hallelujahs ——

"Just follow me." I encouraged the choir, "Do whatever I do and we'll be okay. If I make a mistake, we will all make it together, and for heaven's sake, if you make a mistake, act for all the world as if that is exactly what you meant to do!"

The final run-through of our hardest song went well. The sound man had everything ready…microphones adjusted, monitors in all the right places, recording equipment set… We prayed, and took our places for the Easter service.

Counting was the difficulty with our hardest song. In the choir setting, differences of musical opinion must ultimately be set at the director's feet, and the difficult measure of music was now my baby, so to speak. We would sink or swim on my ability to count correctly. Even the pianist was following my lead. The pressure was on.

Tunnel vision is a problem in directing a cantata. One can be so focused on a particular section, that once that difficulty has been hurdled, the mind can shut down ever so briefly. Such shutdowns seem fatal at the time, but one lives through them, even if one never forgets them.

We breezed through the hard part, and breathed a surreptitious sigh of relief. But the music galloped right along and we were suddenly at a pause in the score. Now we'd been over this piece so many times that it was almost second nature, however the director momentarily lost her wits and during the interlude, sang out, "Hallelujah!" The choir stared at me aghast. Nobody sang while I performed my impromptu solo. Ten measures later, the choir sang their "Hallelujah" just as they had practiced.

No one mentioned my gaffe. There was nothing to say. In a way, that made it even more embarrassing, but time helps take the spotlight off oneself and we go on with life. Of course, the cantata had been recorded, so all is there for the congregation to remember again and again.

A few months after Easter, one of the choir members, who is a good friend, gave me a gift. It was a large cloth bag for carrying my music to and from church. On the satchel were the words, "Practice Random Acts of Kindness." I said thank you and set my music in it, ready to catch up with Johannes and head home. Everyone seemed to be standing around waiting for something, until finally another of the choir members said, "Why don't you look at the other side?"

I did. The other side, in big red letters decorated with a large sequined flower said, "Sing random Hallelujahs."

—— Hormones ——

Depression had set in for the duration. I was so thankful that Johannes was through with his medical-school studies, and that we had this last month before his graduation together. I needed all the moral support I could get, and he needed the rest before beginning his residency.

"I think we should go out to lunch," he said smiling. He had already determined that he would specialize in endocrinology – the study of hormones – and that was a wonderful thing for a woman as pregnant as I was. He was so understanding, and I was such a basket case. Whenever I would burst into tears, or be unexpectedly emotional, he would just smile and say, "It's just your hormones, dear."

Off we went to have lunch. The baby was so huge that there was little room for food, but the thought was what counted, and I appreciated his kindness and care.

There were only booths, which was embarrassing since I was so big and could barely squeeze into the seat. My belly pushed against the table as I sat. We ordered our sandwiches and a nice chocolate milkshake to share. When the waitress brought our food, I took one look at my sandwich and burst into tears. Not just a little quiet tear, but an uncontrolled flood. I had ordered a grilled ham and cheese, and she had brought me a cold sandwich with ham, cheese, lettuce and tomato. A tragic mistake.

The people in the booth across from ours glowered at Johannes, thinking that he had obviously said something hurtful to me. The waitress walked by our table and glared at him accusingly. It never occurred to her that all this upset was over a silly sandwich. I was too overcome with emotion to tell her of her mistake, and Johannes was too embarrassed to say a word – the whole thing was so ridiculous. We drank our milkshake and left.

The Totaled Woman

About two weeks later – the baby was now a week overdue – I was even bigger, and my sweet husband was still very understanding. "Let's try lunch at that restaurant again." he suggested, "I'm sure we'll have a much better time this time, and I'll make sure they get your sandwich right."

Believe it or not, we had the same waitress, who obviously remembered us and seated us at the same booth. With a gasp, I shoved my considerable self into the seat, and she brought us two large glasses of ice water. There was no way I was ordering a ham sandwich again, so I perused the menu as I picked up my glass of ice water. My grasp loosened and it fell to the table sending the entire glassful, ice and all, into Johannes' lap.

"Oooh, I'll bet that's cold!" chuckled the waitress, as she appeared with a towel. Apparently, she felt that I was paying him back for whatever mean thing he had done to me the last time we were there, and she was pleased with my technique.

Johannes explained to me later – after he had a chance to change into some dry clothes – that hormones cause relaxation of the muscles, and that is why I lost my grip on the water glass. Yes, it is wonderful being married to an endocrinologist. After all, it's just hormones.

—— Vibration ——

For some years, I played the piano for Bible Study Fellowship. It was good practice, and the ladies seemed to enjoy singing and hearing the old hymns. I forget what impending crisis caused me to have my cell phone set on vibrate and strapped to my waist that particular day, but in our family there is always an impending crisis.

In the middle of a song, my hip began to vibrate, causing me to skip a few notes. Fortunately, the ladies were singing lustily, and didn't notice the lack of piano. At the end of the singing, I hustled out into the hall. I had missed the call, but there was a message. I knew it couldn't be from the kids, because they all knew that Mom was busy at Bible study on Monday mornings.

"This is the animal veterinary clinic calling," the voice explained, "and we just wanted you to know that Purry's spay went well. She is in recovery now, and you can pick her up after 4:00 this afternoon."

Our cat's name is Bilbo. He is a male, and he's been fixed for quite some time. Daughter Ingrid had left our number for some reason I have never understood. They had just acquired a new kitten – Purry – who obviously was now an 'it'. I called Ingrid before going back in to the Bible study and told her that Purry was doing fine.

"Oh, thanks, Mom, I'll pick her up this afternoon."

Why the veterinarian called me I have no clue. Johannes says I am the pulse-beat of the nation, which seems to be the case.

—— A Fine Day in June ——

The baby was due June 1st. My mom was a real trooper, and had flown out to help me when each of the previous kids had been born, and was planning to help this time too. The problem was, she had been called for jury duty, and since she was not the one having the baby, the court was reticent to excuse her.

Mom was persuasive, explaining her daughter's plight: a physician husband whose hours at the hospital were considerable, and three little children under the age of seven. The court relented with the understanding that she would serve her duty upon her return. My dad was a good sport to let her go for what we all knew would be no more than a week — just until I could get my act together with a new baby.

All our babies came late, so we weren't at all worried that Mom couldn't get a flight until the second week in June. She arrived just in time to wish Johannes bon voyage, as he left for the International Endocrine Meetings. The baby was due June 1st, Mom arrived June 7th and Johannes left for a week of meetings on June 13th.

My mother couldn't believe it. "Can you promise me she won't have this baby before you return?" Johannes was confident, my mother was skeptical. Helping out after the baby comes is one thing, dealing with labor and delivery plus watching three little kids was something else again.

By the time Johannes returned from the meeting, it was June 20th. Mom had put off her jury duty as long as she could, and finally had to fly home on the 22nd. Still no baby.

On a fine day in June – June 27th to be precise – we welcomed a 10-pound baby boy. God's timing was not what we expected, or even wanted, but little Stefan was worth waiting for, and we are thankful.

—— Sleepwalker ——

Nathan was a sleepwalker. As a little boy, we had to be vigilant at night, making sure he didn't fall down the stairs, walk out the front door or meet with disaster in the bathroom.

As he approached his teen years, he was still a sleepwalker, only now it was harder to secure the premises to assure his safety. He could unlock doors in his sleep, and we worried about his opening the door of the house, and falling into the creek in the back yard.

The tricky thing about sleepwalkers is that they have their eyes open, and look for all the world as if they are awake. We could always tell when Nathan was asleep though, because he did everything double-speed, like the old silent movies.

As we were getting ready for bed one night, we heard a noise in the garage. Just as Johannes went to check it out, Nathan burst through the door that led to the garage and sprinted down the stairs, taking a fast lap around the family room before going into his bedroom and slamming the door. When we checked on him, he was in bed fast asleep.

The last time Nathan walked in his sleep is a day he will probably always remember. Johannes and I were relaxing in the upstairs living room. The foyer was six steps down, and was open to view, with only a wrought-iron railing at the edge of the living room. Nathan's bedroom was down six more steps in the lower level. The stairs were to the right, the front door was to the left.

I heard a noise in the foyer, and walked over to see if the dog was at the front door. As I leaned over the railing and peered toward the front door, Nathan came racing quickly but quietly up the stairs. Since my head was turned toward the door, I had no idea there was anyone in the foyer until something caught the corner of my eye.

I gasped. Johannes – thinking we had an intruder in the house – picked up one of the dining-room chairs and raced toward the foyer. Nathan woke up to see his father coming at him, brandishing the chair like a weapon. He burst into tears, and sat down on the floor, totally bewildered.

That is the last time Nathan went sleepwalking. I guess he was sufficiently scarred that from then on he dealt with his dreams only in the safety of his bed.

—— Condemned By Human Ears ——

We finally realized that if we were going to get any sleep, we'd have to move upstairs. Our bedroom was next door to Nathan's, and we hadn't had a good night's sleep in weeks.

In making this move, we realized that Ingrid would have to take the room next to Nathan's, but we hoped that a youngster would be more adaptable than her parents, and that she would be able to adjust. Adjust to what, you ask.

There were two difficulties. Nathan was what one might call 'a thrasher'. Variously throughout the night, he would hurl himself into the wall as he turned over in his bed. We moved his bed to the far side of the room, and that handled that problem. The other problem was harder to solve.

We have a musical family. All the children sing. They sing together, separately, whatever. We love music. If we have a star singer, however, it is Nathan. This is good, this is something special in Nathan's life, this is the problem. Nathan sings in his sleep…not quiet lullabies or little children's songs, but songs with gusto…*Columbia, the Gem of the Ocean*, *Battle Hymn of the Republic*, *America the Beautiful*. Our older son is a patriotic young man, but how many 8-year-olds do you know who even know those songs, let alone sing them in their sleep?

One night, about midnight, Nathan was in full voice. As he started on verse three of *America the Beautiful* — it was easy to hear the words through the bedroom wall — he sang, "Thine alabaster cities gleam, Condemned by human ears!" The correct words, of course, are "Undimmed by human tears." So, we moved upstairs. Nathan continued to sing, but Ingrid slept right through it.

Nathan is now married, and I have often wondered, does his little boy sing in his sleep? Our kid grew up, and we don't have to worry about it anymore. Sometimes we sigh, missing those days when our children were young, and we worried about stuff like singing and banging the wall. Worries get bigger as the kids get bigger, you know.

The Lord is able to handle the little stuff and the big stuff, and for that I am truly thankful.

—— I'm Very Disappointed At You ——

In our house, you knew you were in trouble when you heard your middle name. Now, all our kids have very nice middle names, unlike mine, which I endured until I got married and could give it up for my maiden name.

While it is true that we had trouble agreeing on a name for our second son, fearing that we would have to bring him home from the hospital with 'Hey You' written on his birth certificate, Stefan does have two very handsome names. I seemed to use them both often when he was a toddler.

"Stefan Marcus, what are you doing? Stefan Marcus, come here right now. Stefan Marcus…"The Marcus was the operative word, and Stefan knew it.

One morning, Stefan was as exasperated with his mother as she was with him. Instead of cleaning up his toys in his room, he walked down the hall to the kitchen, looked at me sternly, and stomped his foot, "Mommy Marcus," he said, "I am very disappointed at you."

Funny how little ones seem to think they are on a level equal with their parents. When Mommy says, "I want you to take a nap now." the toddler is not at all phased and responds, "But I don't want to take a nap." As if that answers the topic completely. Daddy says, "Pick up your toys now." The child answers, "You pick them up, I'm busy." No disrespect is meant, a little one just doesn't understand his position in the family structure.

When the Lord speaks to me, how do I answer? I'm afraid I often remind myself of my little kids. My Father is on a much higher plane, and I need to remember that when I speak with Him.

—— You Didn't Trust Me ——

Peer pressure is difficult for teens to deal with. We struggled with our kids as they struggled with acceptance by their peers. They never really fit in with the crowd. This problem was partly our "fault," and was something we were privately proud of. We took pride in seeing each one, according to the personality involved, stand up and refuse to go along when the group was proposing something wrong, or just plain stupid.

When Stefan was just starting high school, he and his buddies decided to go to the movies. They had been mowing lawns over the summer, and had their own money to spend. It took some time to decide which movie was worthy of their hard-earned cash, and Stefan let me know which one they had chosen. I looked it up on the Christian movie guide, and suggested that they choose another one that was more suitable for young teens.

Boy, mothers have no idea about the real world...

I dropped the boys off at the theater – actually several theaters in one – and watched for them to choose the theater that had the show Stefan told me they were going to see; one he and I had discussed and we had approved.

They turned toward the wrong theater. I got out of the car, and followed them into the theater, explaining to the manager that I wouldn't need a ticket, since I would be right out with my son.

Stefan was mortified. On the way home he said, "You call Grandmother and ask her, Mom. She wouldn't have done what you did."

I called my mom, pretty sure that she would be right on my wavelength. After all, she'd reared a son, and knew how it was. "It seems to me that you didn't trust Stefan. After all, he was spending his own money." she said, "If it had been me, I suppose I would have waited until he got home, and then discussed it with him privately instead of embarrassing him in front of his friends."

"I told you so, Mom," Stefan said triumphantly after I told him what Grandmother had said, "I knew Grandmother would understand."

While it is true that after I dragged him out of the theater, we never had an honesty issue like that again, I am sorry I handled it the way I did. At some point, a parent has to relinquish some control and allow the children to make some mistakes. Perhaps this time, the mistake was mine.

—— Another Movie ——

Ingrid's boyfriend, Jeff, was not a believer, and in our home this was a problem. She and her dad struggled for two years while she rebelled in her quiet way and her father stood fast for what was right. As an adult, now married to a fine Christian man, she has thanked her dad more than once for standing firm, but at the time, the home waters were choppy.

"I'm meeting Jessica at the theater, Mom. We're going to see the new Batman movie. I'll be home pretty early, but you don't need to wait up for me." She took her dad's car, and off she went.

About an hour after she left, the phone rang. "Hello, Mrs. Veldhuis? This is Jessica, is Ingrid there? I was wondering if she'd like to come over to my house, and we could just hang out tonight."

The jig was up. After a brief consultation with Johannes, I jumped in the car and headed for the theater. Having no idea where she was for sure, I guessed that she was with Jeff watching the Batman film. As I pulled up to the theater, I saw Johannes' car in the parking lot.

At the ticket window, I explained that I was merely entering the theater to retrieve my daughter. The theater was dark, but a determined mother has capabilities beyond the norm. I could pick Ingrid out with little trouble, even in a full theater. There was an empty seat next to Jeff's, so I sat down, leaned over and said, "Jeff, Ingrid will be leaving now."

Being a parent isn't all it's cracked up to be sometimes. I'm not sure who was more miserable driving home that night – the daughter caught in a lie, or the parent who caught her.

—— Daddy Needs a BandAid ——

We lived in the country, and Daddy was off in the woods with the kids gathering kindling for the fireplace. They returned sooner than I expected, and Nathan bolted through the front door.

"Mom! I need a Kleenex! Dad hurt himself, and he needs a Kleenex."

"What happened to Dad?" I asked as I handed Nathan a couple of tissues.

"Oh, he banged his head, but he's okay." Nathan tore back out the door.

Olivia was the next one in the door. "Mommy, I need a cup of water! Daddy wants me to bring him a cup of water." I gave her a cup of water with a top so our little girl wouldn't spill it on the way outside.

Next Stefan slammed the door. "Mommy, can I get a pillow for Daddy?"

"A pillow, Stefan? What is the matter with Daddy?" Our 5-year-old looked serious, "He has a cut on his head, but he's okay, Mom." I handed him a pillow from the couch, and went back to dinner preparations.

"Mom! Where are the BandAids? Dad needs a BandAid!"

"Ingrid, if Dad has a cut on his head, why do you need a BandAid? It will just stick to his hair."

"I need to help him stop the bleeding," our oldest daughter persisted.

It was obviously time to see what was really going on with the kindling brigade. I found Johannes sitting on the cement, propped up against the garage door, white as chalk. His little ministering spirits fluttered around him, aware that all was not right with their big strong dad.

After we helped him inside to a comfortable easy chair, the story unfolded. He had tried to pull down an old dead branch from one of the trees. It was quite a ways above his head, and as he pulled, the entire top of the dead tree snapped in two, striking him on the head and nearly knocking him unconscious. With the children's eager but ineffectual assistance, he staggered as far as the garage where he sat down. He almost fainted, but was able to slump into a sitting position before that happened.

I tried to remove any pieces of wood embedded in his scalp, but doctoring is definitely not my thing. I suggested the emergency room, but my doctor husband had no intention of staggering into the ER where everyone would know him, and would ask him what had happened. So Johannes removed small remnants of the tree from his scalp for more than a month.

The kids had tried to help, but their knowledge was that of children. If their love could have fixed the problem, he would have been healed instantly. Unfortunately, while their love helped heal his spirit, only time helped heal his head.

—— Thank You, Mr. Edison ——

Alisson was in fourth grade. She was sensitive and intelligent; but for the last two years, she had frustrated her teachers. We were now half-way through fourth grade, and I was at her parent-teacher conference.

"Alisson can't just sit and listen in class." complained her teacher, "She is always looking around, or checking under her desk, or writing in her little notebook. She is a straight-A student, but she is a frustrating pupil."

As a teacher in the same school, I dreaded walking down the halls, just in case I would meet her teacher, who would tell me another story of Alisson's lack of attention in the classroom. It had been that way in the third grade, and here we were facing it again.

The fourth grade was embarking on a biography research project. The selection of the famous person she was to research fell at a time when Alisson was with her Dad on a visit to her cousins in Florida. I had to do the picking. All the famous women had been taken by other students, so I looked over the list and selected Thomas Edison, having no idea if Alisson would be interested in him.

She was at first disappointed that her person was a man, but she recovered from her upset, and set out to read about this unusual man who invented so many things, including the light bulb.

"Mommy, did you know that Thomas Edison only went to school until the third grade? Maybe I could quit school too!"

She didn't quit the fourth grade. She completed her project, and it changed her life. As she put the finishing touches on her poster and showed us the paper she had written, she smiled and said, "I'm okay, Mom! I'm just like Thomas Edison."

—— A Precious Memory ——

Johannes was in his third year of medical school, and our sporty red Chevy was on its last legs. After all, it had almost 100,000 miles on it when we got married — and we'd been married three years now.

My folks were buying a new car and offered us Dad's old business car, which was high-mileage, but in excellent condition. They drove it across the country from Idaho to Pennsylvania, and then treated us to a Broadway play and a night at the Waldorf Astoria in New York City. (Life before kids allowed such extravagance.) The new car drove like a dream.

The drive back to Hershey was fun. Mom and I were chatting in the back seat; Johannes was driving, while he and Dad discussed whatever interested them. Now, the New Jersey Turnpike is a scary stretch of road under any conditions, but this day it was raining, which made the driving even more nerve wracking.

Suddenly, we heard a loud bang. All the lights on the instrument panel flashed, and the car immediately lost power. We limped over onto the shoulder of the highway and lurched to a stop. As the men got out of the car, traffic careened over the hill, bent upon destruction — our destruction.

Mom and I weren't worried; we knew our men could fix any problem. "Wouldn't it be funny," I said, "if they walked to the back of the car carrying the fan in their hands. It would make a great cartoon for the funny papers. Of course, it would never happen, but that's what would make it so funny."

At that very moment, Johannes and Dad walked toward the back of the car... Johannes had the engine fan in his hands...

We waited over an hour for a tow truck, but we were finally on our way to Trenton where there was a mechanic who would be able to repair the damage the fan had done when it hurled out of its mooring and slashed through the radiator. The towing arrangement meant that we were actually riding on the bed at the back of a large wrecker truck. This meant that when we got to the toll booth, the truck driver paid his toll, and then pulled up enough for Johannes to reach down from the back of the truck and pay our toll. We were only slightly humiliated.

Since Johannes had to be back for class the next day, we rented a car. Mom and Dad spent the night in Trenton and drove the car back to Hershey the following evening after the major repairs. They were so glad to hop a plane and get back home.

While it was an expensive and frustrating trip for my folks, we really did have a lovely time together. We drove that old Pontiac for many years – long after we had kids. Not all precious memories are of the good times; some of the most priceless come from the hard times in our lives. This was one of those memories.

── I Knew She Was Dying ──

Olivia had just turned two. Johannes was in Australia. I had promised the children that we would drive from Hershey to Virginia Beach to visit some dear friends, since Daddy would be gone for two weeks. One problem was Olivia had the flu. Another problem was I had promised our five- and six-year-olds that we would go. The last problem was I possessed very limited common sense.

Our dear pediatrician was concerned: Olivia had not eaten any solid food in almost two weeks, and had not been able to even hold down liquids for the last five days. "She might need some intravenous fluids if she isn't better by tomorrow," he told me.

That night, she ate half of a baby biscuit, and I knew she was cured. So I packed up the suitcases, loaded the car, and the next morning we took off for Virginia Beach. As we drove, Olivia became sicker and sicker. After three or four hours, even I realized I had made a terrible mistake. There was no use to turn around, since we were more than half-way there; but I truly believed she would die before we arrived at our friends' house.

The Totaled Woman

She was still alive when we drove into their driveway. I carried her into the house and called our pediatrician in Hershey. Of course, looking back on it all, that was really dumb…I mean what was he going to be able to do from there…but as I have said before, wives of physicians are fairly useless in medical crises.

The moment I heard his voice on the phone, I burst into tears, sobbing uncontrollably for some time. I'm sure he thought Olivia had died, and I was sure she was going to. When I was able to gasp out the problem, he said calmly, "Now Marcia, you need to find a hospital. She needs intravenous fluids, and this will fix the problem."

Olivia recovered nicely, but her mother has never quite gotten over it. Actually, my stupidity almost caused the death of our child. Sure, I lacked the common sense of a toad, but I really don't think that was the biggest problem. I never sought the Lord before I made the decision to take the trip. It never occurred to me that I needed to, after all, she did eat half a biscuit.

Lord, keep me on my knees. My family needs me in that position.

—— Snow ——

The sullen sky is sulking; it is silent.
No rumbling sound escapes to tell its plan.
A comforter of gray spreads o'er the even,
And hides from earthly view the heaven's intent.

As quiet as the night before the morn
A change, so subtle, thrills my weary eye
As feathers from the comforter fall freely;
Gray no more, white innocence is born.

No whirling wind, no rankling thunder roll
Can mar the purity of white without.
A soundless plea cries deep within my being
For feathers white within my very soul.